Praise

'Lisa Turner's personal trauma and the resulting debilitating impact drove her to try multiple healing modalities and to developing her very own modality in a determined search for what works. In this illuminating book she unveils why we get stuck and how beliefs create our circumstances and experiences. Dr Turner's signature CET modality is the answer so many of us are seeking in order to open up to the life-giving energy of love in all its forms and finally heal from our addictions, avoidance patterns and so much more, and find blessed release.'

— **Susan Glusica**, multi-international bestselling author and Money Master Coach, Unrivaled Realizations LLC

'The #1 most critical key to your success and happiness is mastering your mind and emotions and Lisa's new book *CET Yourself Free* is a must read on the topic. If you fail to master your mind and emotions you could be set up for a life of struggle and misery. Don't miss this essential book! Get it now and start reading it immediately.'

— **Christian Mickelsen**, bestselling author, 4 Time Inc. 5000 award winner, and Coaching Industry Leader

'Lisa's commitment not only to helping others process emotional trauma and experiences but also to deeply understand the root causes and fundamentals of exactly how to leverage her CET System is inspiring. This book opens the possibility for truth, healing and individual empowerment. The balance of her love, quick wit and genius at work is present with every turn of the page.'

— **Kaci Brown**, bestselling author, speaker, Soul Aligned Business Consultant, Freedom To Impact Co-Founder

'Emotional freedom is essential if you want to succeed beyond your wildest expectations. Yet until now, there hasn't been a clear path for "getting unstuck" that includes both psychology *and* the hidden spiritual toolkit that is a part of every individual's birthright. That's what's so exciting about CET. Lisa has truly made simple the process of transforming emotional energy and using it for success. While there are a lot of teachers out there who promise to "turn on" your connection to your Higher Self, Lisa is one of the few who has the process down to a science – literally! Read this book and turn on powers you didn't even know you had.'

— **Elizabeth Purvis**, Founder, 7-Figure Goddess® and Feminine Magic®

'This book is full of revolutionary insights into the world of our emotions – insights that will change your perspective on everything from friendships to family dynamics, romance and even what makes us happy. It's not your emotions that are the problem. They're actually just symptoms of what's really going on in your life – the real problems, the ones that need to be solved. And this book is going to teach you how to identify those problems so that you can solve them once and for all!'

— **Maria Czyzynska**, CET practitioner

'What makes us feel the way we feel? It's a question that has plagued humanity for millennia but one that science has only recently begun to answer. In *CET Yourself Free*, Lisa offers a mind-blowing explanation of how emotions work. She explains in clear, simple language how the brain processes feelings, and she gives examples of what happens in the brain when we experience them. This book will change the way you think about your own life – and it may even change the way you live it!'

— **Shefton Somersall-Weekes**, CET practitioner

CET Yourself Free

Change your life with the gentle alchemy of Conscious Emotional Transformation

Dr Lisa Turner

R^ethink

With Love
Lisa

Author's Note

This book explains how CET (Conscious Emotional Transformation) works and how it differs from other emotional healing methods and therapies. If you already have something that works, *great!* Keep using it, but it does beg the question as to why you've reached for this book. CET works on a completely different premise to other therapies. If you have trained in and offer another modality mentioned in this book, note that I am in no way intending to dismiss your technique or skills. I am simply offering a deeper and alternative understanding of another modality.

CET, as referred to throughout this book, stands for Conscious Emotional Transformation and is completely distinct from Cognitive Enhancement Therapy.

A note on the case studies and clients mentioned in this book: the clients' permissions were requested and granted before including them in this book. All names and personal details have been changed to protect the privacy of the clients, even those who were willing to be referred to personally.

Where I describe my personal experiences, the names have been changed to protect the identities of those involved.

Contents

Prologue

In a small corner office in the Faraday Tower at Southampton University, I listened to Professor Tidmarsh, following his line of reasoning carefully. As he landed his final point, I realised with a sinking feeling that he had just elegantly destroyed the foundation of my entire PhD thesis.

I was in the final live viva of my PhD assessment. Four years of working every weekend and evening. Four years of personally funded fees that added up to more than my flat had cost.

I took a moment to think through his points again. He can't be right, can he? Did I miss something? The world started to shrink. I started to panic. How could I have missed something so fundamental? If I didn't think of something, it would wipe out years of hard work.

I'd have to start almost from scratch again. Professor Tidmarsh sat in silence as I thought and thought and thought.

I gazed out through the windows across the waters of the Solent. A soft ray of sunlight struggled out from behind a blanket of low cloud and caught the surface of the water. As it shone back at me, I went into another dimension. I started at the beginning of my mathematical model, laying it all out in my mind: the sequence of assumptions, the symbols, calculus, rules, trigonometric identities and engineering formulae seemed to glide past. I watched and manipulated the concepts silently on my mental screen. Suddenly, one of the formulae shone brighter. It grew. I re-read it on my mind-screen and realised David Tidmarsh was wrong.

I said, 'Have you considered that this is a NACA series 4 aerofoil? And the dimensions you're describing are more like – well, a brick or a bus. If we apply this aspect ratio to the model…' I patted my pockets for a pen but the only one within reach was in his top suit pocket. I took it and re-wrote the formula with the correct aspect ratio. I described how this could not be solved analytically and that a numerical method was needed. Pausing only to check what seven multiplied by eight was (I've never managed to learn my times tables), I concluded my walk-through to the final solution.

He looked at me and broke into a huge grin. 'Well done. You saw my trap and avoided it beautifully. Nice work (he paused), Dr Austin.'

I re-ran those words in my mind. Doctor. *Doctor* – a title conferred only on those who had been awarded a PhD. I was speechless. I had done it. I wasn't always sure I could do it, but despite everything, I had.

When I was first learning calculus, I was in Gary's flat wrangling with a maths problem. 'Let me help,' he said. I showed him the problem, not for a moment thinking he didn't know how to do this level of maths. He'd always insisted that he was so much more intelligent than I was. He couldn't do the problem, but he didn't admit this to me. Instead, he got angry and told me I must have written the problem down wrong because it was unsolvable. He said, 'You're so stupid. You can't do maths. You'll never be able to do maths.' Unfortunately, I believed him. Those words had planted themselves in my unconscious mind and grown strong roots. I continued to believe I was stupid. I stopped trying to do maths.

I finally worked through these limiting beliefs and overcame them to get my degree in engineering, but they did prevent me from taking my first choice of degree subject: physics. If I'd had access to CET, I would have saved myself so much hard work and heartache. Now, I'm working towards a masters in quantum physics. Maths has changed from a panic-inducing struggle to just being a bit of a challenge. I no longer feel that panic of not being able to understand. Maths is like a complex puzzle which I enjoy. I still don't know my tables – but I do have a PhD in mathematical modelling and aero-acoustics.

Introduction: Love Letter To My Reader

Dear Reader – I want to start by saying, 'I love you.'

I know. It's an unconventional way to start a book, but if nothing else, I tend towards the unconventional.

You might find it strange that I'm saying I love you. You might be wondering, 'What does this mean?' You might be thinking, 'But you don't even know me!' For me, that's not how love works. As you'll see through this book, I have a different view of love.

For now, just know that you are loved unconditionally.

I love you for picking up this book.

I love you for reading it, or for not reading it.

I love you for applying what you'll learn here, or not.

I love you, no matter what.

I don't need to know you or anything about you to love you.

Who am I?

Who is this stranger who expresses love for you and why should you even listen to me?

My name is Lisa; Dr Lisa Turner PhD, BEng, CEng. I am the founder of MindCET, a spiritual and consciousness awakening organisation that specialises in training professional coaches and practitioners. I'm also an engineer and a scientist: I hold a real PhD in aero-acoustics and mathematical modelling. How does an engineer become a therapist, healer and spiritual teacher? It's true; it's an unusual transition.

It didn't happen all at once. It began with my search to heal myself. As I found modalities that were effective, I initially trained as a practitioner for my own benefit. Then I started offering services to those who asked. For a while, I led a double life: I was 'Mrs Turner the shamanic healer' in the evenings and at weekends, and 'Dr Austin, the senior lecturer and researcher in engineering' by day. In 2004, I finally started my first spiritual development business teaching people how to connect to their higher selves. As I learned more about how to remove 'blocks' for both spiritual development and healing trauma, the process I outline here emerged and evolved into the powerful modality it is today: CET.

My core belief is that everyone can be, and deserves to be, free from pain and trauma from the past. This should, and *can*, be quick and comfortable. I developed CET after being groomed, trafficked and then kept as a house prisoner for five years in my teens by a paedophile. I escaped, but had post-traumatic stress disorder (PTSD), agoraphobia, social anxiety disorder and deep feelings of worthlessness and depression that affected every waking moment of my life. I tried every therapy available, from the wild and woo-woo to the highly academic. Through research and plenty of trial and error, I found what works and, more importantly, *why* it works. This book shares the research, the journey and the results of developing a spiritual technology that enables anyone to be free from their painful past. CET makes this possible.

As an engineer, I approach healing and spirituality not from theory, but from what works. In explaining what works, I occasionally reference scientific principles, but you don't need a PhD to understand this book. I try to make my ideas as sound as possible, based on logical reasoning and what's useful. Where there is science, I'll reference and explain it, but I make no claims about the absolute truth of any of the ideas or principles in this book. I'm less interested in dogma and 'truth' and more interested in *what works*. If it's useful and it works, I apply it.

Engineers love simple, easy to use, elegant and powerful solutions. We like things to work. To be practical. To be useable. This is exactly what you'll learn in this book.

Who are you?

Now that you know who I am, who are you?

If you're like many people, sometimes you find life a minefield, a battleground or a wasteland. Like many, you might feel as if you're grasping for a tiny amount of a happiness that regularly eludes you. We instinctively know this isn't how life should be, but this is how many of us experience it. This sad state is only one of the things I want to transform in this book.

I imagine that you might fall somewhere within these two groups of people. Because I'm a geek who loves diagrams, I suggest you map yourself into a Venn diagram: you might find yourself in the middle (ie, in *both* groups).

Healers

You might be a coach, healer, therapist or some kind of practitioner working with clients. It may be that you've sat toe-to-toe with a distressed client who has associated into a traumatic memory from the past. While she weeps, cries and sobs, you look on in agonising, helpless empathy. The overwhelming feeling you have is: 'I want to help.'

It's likely you have one or a range of tools and skills that you use to assist those experiencing emotional pain from their past. There are certainly a lot out there: Reiki, emotional freedom technique (EFT), matrix re-imprinting, hypnosis, neurolinguistic programming (NLP), psychic work, energy healing, counselling, coaching, Time Line Therapy™, shamanic healing, spiritual healing and so on. The list goes on, and these are all *great* tools. They all work, but have you noticed that sometimes your clients come back and they still have the same problem? They repeat the same story. They still slip back into the past trauma. They can't ever seem to completely let it go, or they have slightly different problems. New ones keep surfacing. It starts to feel like a game of 'whack-a-mole' or painting the Forth Road bridge: you know you're making some progress, but it's hard to see where it ends…If it ends. It's like you're never quite getting to the Source.

You're left wondering, 'What's the point of trying to help people? What's the point of being a healer or a coach?' Maybe you've even begun to despair. I've met many healers and therapists who are simply burned out with empathy fatigue. They're exhausted from feeling what their clients feel and knowing there must be a better way to help in a deep and lasting way. If this sounds like you, you're in the right place.

Seekers

You might be seeking relief from emotional pain. You know these painful emotions are from the past, based on a variety of symptoms. You might have low self-confidence or self-esteem. You might have deep feelings of unworthiness. Maybe you struggle to assert yourself or ask for what you want. You find yourself overreacting to minor events, or small slights or criticism might hit you like a truck. Events in the present trigger flashbacks and can send you into a spiral of emotional turmoil. Logically, you probably know that these emotional responses are unwarranted, but you still feel them and no matter how hard you try to suppress them, they come back time and again.

You may even have an in-depth understanding and knowledge of the cause of these problems and fully recall the past events that led to them, but like a car mechanic diagnosing an engine fault, until a repair is undertaken, the problem persists. You may work hard at overcompensating for your feelings, leaving you exhausted and drained. Perhaps your inner world affects your outer world in the form of abusive relationships, underemployment or eating disorders... Unchecked, our emotions can eventually wreak havoc on our physical bodies, triggering cascades of stress hormones, suppressing our immune systems and leading to more serious conditions.

Just as those in the healers' group have trained in a plethora of healing modalities, you might have been on the receiving end of therapy, treatment and healing techniques, trying one after another in the hope that *this* one will work. It's likely that many have had some impact, but none have really solved the root cause permanently, so you continue your quest, silently seeking release from your pain. Good news. This book is for you.

It's also likely you fall into *both* groups. You may be a wounded healer seeking relief for yourself, but also (out of love, compassion and empathy) desiring to share this healing with others who need it as much as you do. Whichever group you're in, you're in the right place.

You aren't broken. You don't need fixing

Many healing modalities work from the basis that you are broken and need fixing. I disagree. Unresolved emotional pain from the past can impact all of our interpersonal relationships.[1] It can limit us in our careers

---

1. B Badenoch, *The Heart of Trauma: Healing the embodied brain in the context of relationships (Norton Series on Interpersonal Neurobiology)* (WW Norton & Company, 2017)

and jobs. We might not get promotions or make those all-important sales calls. Emotional pain can lower our confidence, stifle our creativity and prevent us taking appropriate risks, while triggering us to take risky gambles. It can even impact our physical health[2] by suppressing our immune system and flooding our bloodstream with excess stress hormones. This creates a cascade of physical problems from weight gain, insomnia and low energy to increased recovery time from illnesses. That's why 'releasing' emotions is so important to our wellbeing.

I want you to know, first and foremost, that it's not your fault. You've done nothing wrong, and there's nothing wrong with you. You've simply lacked the right tools for the job. Think of it this way: if you want to chop down a tree, a screwdriver won't be much use. To fell a tree, an axe works better than a screwdriver. A chainsaw is even better than an axe. If you prefer a less violent-sounding metaphor: it's as if you have been trying to boil a kettle by shouting at it. Your voice won't cause the kettle to boil. Plugging it in and switching on the power to the heating element will work much better.

In this paradigm-busting book, I'll share with you the discoveries that helped me make sense, not only of my own emotional pain, but also the nature and purpose of emotions themselves. You'll discover an entirely

---

2.   L Feldman Barrett, *How Emotions Are Made: The secret life of the brain* (Pan Books, 2017)

new way of thinking about emotions. You'll learn about trauma (with a small 't') and how events from the past can haunt our present, but more importantly, you'll learn that they can be released so you are free from your emotional pain.

It's easy to confuse the past with the emotions attached to it. I've been there, so I know how it can feel to believe that nothing and no one can help, that things won't change and that experiencing love and healing just isn't possible for you. However, because I've been there and tried anything and everything to bring myself back from the brink of despair and hopelessness, I also know what works, what works just a little, and what doesn't work at all.

This book introduces an entirely new paradigm for healing trauma. CET is a psycho-spiritual healing technology that accomplishes in a matter of hours what other therapies might take years to achieve (if at all). CET evolved from my realisation that all of our modern healing modalities could be sorted into two categories: those that approached releasing emotions psychologically and those that approached releasing emotions spiritually. Complete and permanent change needs both. I knew we needed an entirely different process for recovery – one that addressed the psychological *and* the spiritual dimensions of trauma and was also quick and easy to use.

There is only love

CET works on a series of unique premises all relating to, and explaining the concept and emotion of, love (you can also call it energy, chi, lifeforce, essence, prana or any other term you feel comfortable with). My book's radical promise to you is simple: love is the only emotion.

If love is the only emotion, why is our world filled with pain? Why do we go to war? Why do people intentionally hurt themselves and others? Why do people act out of selfishness, hatred, greed and fear? Yes, pain is real. Every day we see people behaving in ways that don't serve themselves or others. This doesn't mean that God/the Divine has abandoned us or is punishing us. All the 'bad' we see in the world, in ourselves and in others isn't a sign of a broken universe. Bad behaviours are not proof of a meaningless existence. They are simply examples of resistance to love or love's energy gone astray.

It was from this core belief, with a lot of trial and error, that I discovered CET: a process that turns everything you know about healing on its head. It works on a unique premise – one not used in any other modality. It is a simple, profound, rapid process that allows you to let go of your past and live your brightest, best and most joyful present. Five 'principles of love' form the basis of CET:

Principle 1: There is only one emotion, and that emotion is love. When love flows, this is when we feel love, joy or something positive.

Principle 2: The entire universe is made of energy. This is neither negative nor positive. It is simply energy.

Principle 3: Every individual is an infinite being, with an infinite number of channels through which emotional energy can flow.

Principle 4: The experience we call 'feeling a negative emotion' is caused by the absence of love, or the resistance to love. What we feel as a negative emotion is actually the experience of resisting the flow of love energy.

Principle 5: We are evolving beings, always growing and changing for the better. This fifth principle makes CET more than a therapy. It is not only remedial, but also generative. CET is a process for, and of, transformation. CET:

- Finds the resistance to energy
- Removes *all* resistance
- Releases entire histories of trauma
- Rebalances the backlog of energy
- Creates new neural pathways that allow more energy to flow

- Returns us to Source

As you make your way through this book, I'll keep coming back to and unpacking these five principles. Here's a quick summary of my most important concepts:

Ideally, love should flow freely and infinitely throughout your entire being. Why? Because you are an infinite being, with an infinite number of energy channels or neurological pathways.

Your infinite being expresses itself in three distinct but interconnected parts: your conscious mind, your unconscious mind and your Higher Self. Your conscious mind is your logical, rational mind – it is limited to what you are aware of. Your unconscious mind is incredibly powerful – it houses your memories and emotions. Although we often aren't aware of the unconscious mind, our choices, beliefs and behaviours reflect its inner workings. Your Higher Self is the part of you that is divine, infinite, pure Source (this is the term I use for what you experience as the highest level of yourself. God, super-consciousness and one-ness with the universe are all alternative terms).

When all three parts of the self are integrated, we experience the pure flow of divine love throughout our physical, emotional, mental and spiritual bodies. We are able to process and release trauma and do not live in spiritual or emotional pain. Sometimes, we experience an event which creates a resistance or block. A block is any resistance to love – it is a metaphor for describing how our neurological pathways can become blocked, damaged or constricted by trauma. Blocks make us feel anger, sadness, guilt, hurt or fear. These 'negative' emotions serve a purpose. They alert us to potential blocks; they cue us in to breakdowns in the communication between our Higher Self, our unconscious mind and our conscious mind.

I have developed a model I call the emotional response cycle (ERC), which explains how our negative emotions give us important feedback. In its attempt to make meaning, our unconscious mind creates harmful or restricting beliefs about ourselves that we experience as anger, sadness, guilt, hurt and fear. Outside of our conscious awareness, we don't know they're there, but we experience their effects. We keep feeling the same shitty feelings and experience a pattern of repeating behaviour that doesn't serve us. Even if we try to heal, even if we have the best intentions, if we aren't able to bring unconscious blocks and limiting beliefs into our conscious awareness, we won't heal.

In this book, I'll show you how to spot any damage to your ERC that may be keeping you stuck, triggered, mired in painful emotions, suffering from PTSD, limiting beliefs, flashbacks and other experiences that prevent you from living your life's true purpose. With CET, you can unblock and repair the flow of love throughout your neurology and release all negative emotions and limiting beliefs from the past.

I know that sounds like a really wild and outlandish claim, and you might be thinking:

- This CET thing can't possibly be that good
- She can't possibly be over her past trauma
- This CET thing sounds great, but I've had far worse trauma and it can't work for me

Of course, you're entirely welcome to keep those beliefs, but why would you want to? My guess is, if you're reading this, you *do* want to be free from the pain in your past and you are open to the possibility of total trauma recovery. I invite you to keep reading and keep your mind open, even if it's just a tiny crack, to let in a little light from new ideas.

The practice of CET

Our professional CET practitioners started from where you might be now. They first learned how to release their own emotional pain and trauma, and then went on to train in the methodology so they could become a guide for others. Some came from a background of coaching, healing or other modalities where, despite their good intentions, they didn't find it easy to get significant results. When their clients didn't get the results they hoped for, they kept coming back with the same problem, which was frustrating for both clients and practitioners.

A trained CET practitioner has learned the skills to pinpoint the resistance and blocks that cause so many challenges in people's lives. CET practitioners work gently with clients to reveal the cause of their emotional pain and release it. They go deeper than many therapeutic techniques, which tend to deal only with the surface-level symptoms. CET practitioners achieve profound results in a fraction of the time and go on to become highly sought-after. Most importantly, they know that they are part of a growing community of paradigm-shifting practitioners who make a difference – not only to the lives of their clients but also to the lives that their clients' impact, creating a ripple effect in the world.

Inevitably, for the sake of confidentiality and professionalism, I'm unable to share some of the detail of what happens in sessions with clients. It's also difficult to reduce what transpires into a formula, as so much of the practice entails client and therapist inching forwards in mutual trust to discover blocks and explore ways to resolve them. Responsiveness, insight and experience are the hallmarks of CET practice.

It's my hope that you read this book and realise that there's nothing wrong with you – there never was. Joy and happiness aren't, and shouldn't be, transactional or based on who you are or what you do. Love is an infinite energy Source, which you can tap into and access more joy, more love and more of the kind of life you desire.

When we can release our resistance to love and allow love's divine energy to flow unblocked through our neurology, we not only heal ourselves, but also become part of a global transformation.

ONE
Recognising Trauma

The first time it happened, I didn't know what was going on. I was sitting in a lecture on something I've long since forgotten about. The lecturer droned on, repeating one of his favourite anecdotes to explain his point. We'd heard it many times before. Suddenly, I wasn't in the lecture room. I was in the flat. Gary was in front of me. Shouting. I heard his voice. I felt the abusive energy, the wrath, the force of his words slamming into me.

The lecture ended and the sounds of the other students getting up to leave brought me back into the present, but the pain stayed with me, burning into my chest, my heart and my solar plexus. I managed to make it to the bathroom before I vomited. Being sick was a blessing – it gave me an excuse to withdraw and not interact with my peers. They could understand vomit, but I didn't think they would understand what had just happened. Hell, I didn't understand it. Not only was I in emotional turmoil, but I also felt ashamed of my emotional pain. I didn't have a name for what I was experiencing.

Signs you have trauma

I didn't realise it then, but what I was experiencing was a form of trauma. Trauma is how we describe any event in the past which continues to cause painful emotions in the present. It describes any experience from the past which remains unresolved or incomplete. If you simply recall that event and can feel the emotional pain now, that's a sign that you may have trauma. The flashback that I experienced in that lecture hall happened because I had not yet fully recovered from being held as a house prisoner by Gary, my abusive, paedophile 'boyfriend' during my teen years.

The truth is, trauma affects every area of the brain. It can become a controlling influence in our lives, preventing us from accessing resources. Trauma can render us helpless, overly reliant on others and dependent on painful attachments and dysfunctional relationships. It leads us to distance ourselves and become hyper-self-sufficient, leading to isolation. Trauma makes us deeply lonely (even if we are 'successful') and it distracts us. Trauma impacts our short-term memory and ability to make decisions. Trauma makes it hard to have healthy, loving and long-lasting relationships. It takes energy to have trauma. It takes even more energy to suppress the pain of trauma. It takes energy to hold on to painful emotions. It takes more energy to keep them repressed or suppressed. That's effort and attention that we could be spending on achieving our desires.

Do you have a memory from the past which, as you think about it now, triggers a painful emotion? If you aren't sure if emotional pain from the past is affecting you in the present, ask yourself if you can relate to any of the tell-tale signs:

- **Addictions:** Emotions are often suppressed or anaesthetised out of consciousness through addictions. Smoking, drinking, video games, TV or eating too much will anaesthetise the pain, but cannot solve the underlying problem.

- **Being judgemental:** A person who is overly judgemental gets stuck in black and white thinking. They see the world in absolutes: right or wrong, yes or no. They live by inflexible rules and judge those who do not adhere to these rules negatively. It's easy to see when someone is judging another harshly, but it's less obvious when someone has turned their judgemental gaze inward. The most judgemental people often judge themselves just as harshly (if not more) than others. Finding simple ways to label events, people and circumstances helps to make sense of the world. It's an attempt to apply meaning, even if it is wrong or doesn't work.

- **Being overly rigid:** New situations are challenging for all of us. Most of us have an internal reserve of 'thinking power' that helps get us through challenges, from the most minor (eg, taking a new route to work) to larger ones (eg, moving to a new city), but someone who has experienced trauma may have a low or non-existent reserve. They are using so much mental/emotional/spiritual (and even physical) energy to simply exist, they may have little or nothing left for handling new situations. (Think of it like a computer's operating system running slowly because too many applications are open or there's a backlog of old files that need to be deleted.) For these people, everything has to be similar and familiar so that they don't have to adjust to, or manage, a new situation.

- **Catastrophising:** To catastrophise is to imagine the worst possible outcomes and think them through, even going so far as to plan for them. This is an attempt to find resources and strategies for when things go wrong. The idea is that if you have planned through what might happen (see below), then your neurology is better prepared if it does go wrong. Traumatised people do this because they know they have fewer resources available for coping with unexpected challenges.

- **Controlling behaviour:** When someone tries to take charge of situations or others, it is an attempt to keep themselves safe by avoiding situations that they know will trigger them.

- **Excessive planning:** The need or compulsion to plan things down to the last detail to avoid unexpected changes, surprises and events is an attempt to avoid being triggered.

- **Failure, rejection or attracting bullies:** Do you do all the right things but get the wrong results? Do you seem to be a magnet for bad luck and bad treatment that, logically, you know you don't deserve? There are complex reasons for this. Simply, others tend to respond to the unconscious expectations we have about ourselves. If we expect to be rejected, teased or treated badly, other people seem to respond unconsciously by providing the treatment we have come to expect.

- **Flashbacks:** In an attempt to complete the ERC, the unconscious mind brings past events into your awareness when you are safe. Sadly, the ERC often encounters problems along the way, so we don't get the healing resolution we need.

- **Low or no energy/feeling tired**: It takes energy to carry emotions (that's why it's called emotional *baggage*) and it takes even more energy to suppress them. If you are lacking in energy, need more sleep than most people, or just have no get-up-and-go, you could be suppressing your emotions. Many of my past clients suffered from chronic fatigue syndrome, which disappeared once they released their emotions.

- **Obsessing over the past:** Obsessively replaying past events, discussions or arguments in our minds and brooding over them or re-imagining them playing out differently are all attempts to find a different meaning or identify alternative ways of behaving.

- **Overreactions:** You overreact to small things (this is also known as 'emotional leakage'). Denied in one area of your life, your emotions literally spill out in other areas. If you are irritable, overly sentimental, easily hurt by small things (eg, road rage), these are signs that the emotions from a broken and looping ERC are spilling over into another area.

- **Physical pain or even illness:** Our unconscious mind often communicates with us through pain, illness or physical discomfort. When we ignore our emotions, our unconscious mind tries to get our attention by sending us messages in the form of pain or illness. This is easy to do, because the unconscious mind governs automatic processes like our immune system and muscles, etc. When we pay attention to our suppressed emotions and release them, the physical problems can disappear. This is particularly true of psychosomatic illnesses. That doesn't mean they are not real: the pain and the problem are real, but they are caused by suppressed emotions.

- **People pleasing/being overly flexible:** If you often over-extend yourself trying to please others, it could be the result of trauma related to a fear of rejection or of being hurt, judged or criticised. You will do everything possible to make sure the people around you are happy. Traumatic experiences can create or reinforce limiting beliefs that we are unworthy, that what we want and need doesn't matter or that *we ourselves* don't matter, so we end up putting others' needs above our own.

- **Problems making decisions:** Similar to being overly rigid, if you have problems making decisions, it may be that you are using so much energy simply managing your day-to-day life that you don't have much thinking space left for making decisions. If you have experienced trauma, you may be in a space of hypervigilance – every little thing, even the most benign, may feel like a threat. Your decisions may have become focused solely on avoiding or mitigating dangers (real and perceived). People who have been in abusive relationships may also have been trained to believe that their ideas and opinions don't matter and so they don't trust themselves to make decisions.

- **Short-term memory loss:** When so much of our brain and processing power is focused on avoiding triggers, we experience short-term memory loss and 'brain farts'. With hypervigilance and trauma draining our reserve 'thinking power', we don't remember where we put our car keys that morning or what someone has just said.

- **Trivialising (or even making fun of) our past trauma:** We use these techniques to distance ourselves from unresolved trauma.

- **Emotional sponging:** In abusive relationships, it's common for the victim to become hypervigilant to their abuser's emotional states as a form of protection. This can turn them into an emotional sponge for all, and any, of the moods of others. They may describe themselves as an empath and feel they need protection from the emotions and energy of other people.

If you recognise yourself in any of these, your suppressed emotions are affecting your present, even if you're currently not feeling that emotion. If it's made you concerned that you might be far more traumatised by your past than you imagined, please do not panic. As someone who's experienced trauma, had most of these symptoms, and then released my past to recover, trust me: it is possible to live free from these experiences.

Specialist help

Many people believe that it's disempowering to suggest that someone in pain cannot heal themselves. It's not that we can't heal ourselves. In fact, some of us do, but it is always easier, faster and more comfortable to seek professional help. After all, nobody suggests it is 'disempowering' to see a dentist. For specialised services, we need a specialist. As a specialist, I, Dr Lisa Turner, house prisoner turned engineer turned spiritual practitioner and entrepreneur, am here to tell you: you *can* be free from your painful past, and it can be easy, quick and powerful. How do I know? For that, we have to go back to the beginning...

I loved a paedophile

I lived a happy childhood. My parents emigrated from England to Australia to seek a better life when I was two. Both entrepreneurs, they started a successful software business. Through their hard work and willingness to take risks, the business grew to become an international success. I knew nothing but warm sunshine, beaches, camping trips in the wild Australian bush and sleepovers with my friends. All that changed when I was twelve.

One day, the new young music teacher, Gary, handed me a piece of paper torn from a spiral notebook. He'd written his personal phone number on it. I took the paper, my hands shaking with excitement, but also with nervousness. Teachers never gave out their home numbers. He said that if I ever wanted to talk to him, I should call him up. Being a lively, outgoing and friendly girl (and maybe a bit daring and cheeky), I phoned him that night.

Our calls became a regular occurrence. I called him most nights of the week and we'd speak for hours, chatting about nothing in particular. He would ask me what I was wearing and what I'd done at school that day. My parents didn't know I was calling a teacher and didn't suspect anything. Over time, the calls started to become more intimate. He would share more about what was going on in his life. Eventually, our conversations became flirtatious. Gary began making sexual innuendos. He told me how beautiful I was. Then it became how sexy I was. By then, I was almost thirteen. Being considered 'sexy' by a grown man made me feel grown up.

Over time, our relationship became increasingly sexual. My guitar lessons were replaced by another sort of lesson entirely. Rather than learning music, I was learning to pleasure Gary. I sensed that I had the power to give or withhold pleasure. Eventually, when I was fourteen, Gary took my virginity. By the time my parents started to suspect anything, it was too late. Gary was adamant that he loved me and I believed I was completely in love with him.

In February of 1984, Gary relocated to England and I left my home and family in Australia to be with him.

It may seem hard to believe that my parents allowed this, but they were also taken in by the kind and loving facade Gary had created. He would praise me to them, saying how amazing I was. They believed that we were in love and that he would take care of me.

Gary rented us a squalid flat in London. His demands started to increase. He wanted all of the money that my mother was sending me as an allowance. I couldn't choose what I watched on TV, what I ate or when I slept. Anything I did that made him unhappy was forbidden. Anything I did that made me happy was forbidden. Anything he wasn't part of was forbidden. Around this time, my friends back home stopped writing to me. No one called. I had never felt so lonely.

I had this golden time after school four days a week when I was alone in the flat for a few hours. I had to be careful, though. I had to come straight home from school and not leave the flat again. I wasn't allowed to go out and buy anything, even if we'd run out of milk or bread. Somehow, Gary always seemed to know if I'd been out again. 'Remember, I'm *always* watching you,' he'd say. Gary would withdraw kindness and love when I didn't do what he wanted and lavish me with it when I did. I learned to be the person he wanted me to be. It was a slow, constant drip of emotional and psychological abuse – a form of brainwashing. This was how he trained me to do what he wanted. He became increasingly verbally and emotionally abusive. He'd turn up his amplifier while I was studying, making it impossible to concentrate. He called me stupid, a slut, ugly and big. Sex became brutal and painful. He'd prevent me from experiencing orgasm and shame me when my body didn't react in the way that he wanted. I can remember the greasy stench of his unwashed body pressed against mine when he hit me for the first time.

I started to self-harm. It started with not feeling clean. I was having a bath and I took the nailbrush and I started to scrub my feet. I started to feel pain when the brush caught the edge of some of the thinner, more delicate skin. I was aware of the pain, but I couldn't stop. My hand just kept scrubbing. It hurt, but it felt good to be in control of something. I scrubbed until I bled.

The filthy flat, the ugly wallpaper, the dirty carpet, the putrid smell, the bad food, not being able to do anything I liked, having no choice...And the pain: it came again and again in waves, the pain of self-hatred, shame, utter despair and helplessness. I silently begged for help. *'Please, someone. Anyone. Help me. Someone must come and help me.'* In that moment of despair, the strangest thing happened. From somewhere else in the room, I heard a voice.

The power of choice

The voice screamed, 'No one is coming!' I was shocked. Where had it come from? Who was it? Was I going mad? Had Gary finally sent me insane? As my heart slowed down and my panic and fear subsided, the words of the voice sunk in: 'No one is coming.' First came even more despair. *No one will ever come and rescue me.* Then other thoughts bubbled up:

I had the choice to leave.

I didn't need to wait to be rescued.

I didn't need to wait for help.

I didn't need to be given permission.

I could give up believing that it would get better or I could choose to be free.

And *only* I could choose.

The truth was that escaping Gary's flat wasn't the happy ending that so many might hope or imagine. It took me almost a year after hearing that voice before I could leave, so tightly woven was the energy entanglement between us. Gary had made every decision for me. He chose what I ate, what I wore, what I watched on TV, when I slept and when I did anything – *if* I did anything. He didn't need to bully, shout or command. He had moulded me to obey.

My realisation that he would never change unless I changed something was the key to my decision to leave. The day I stopped pretending that there would ever be equality in our relationship was a step towards my freedom. This was the beginning – the start of a long journey to recover and heal.

TWO
Coping Is Not Enough

I sat at my desk staring up into the ruddy face of Les, the factory foreman, as he loomed over my desk with his voice raised, telling me why he needed me to pack up my test equipment 'right now'. My heart raced and my palms were sweaty as I stammered that I knew I was in the right. The instruction to get the testing up and running had come from the top, the directors, but Les thought he knew otherwise. Squabbles over resources and petty power struggles aren't unusual in business. As the only woman engineer, I was used to men in the hierarchy trying to usurp me. What I was fighting right now was rising panic. The position of technical manager came with a private office, which, frankly, was more of a curse than a blessing. I had privacy, but when I sat at my desk and someone came in to speak to me, I was trapped. I say trapped – in truth,

I simply mean that there was another person between me and the door – but for someone who had been kept as a house prisoner in a highly abusive situation, whenever there was someone between me and the only escape route, it would trigger me.

When I share my experience, people often struggle to understand how someone can feel so threatened in a normal situation. The full story is in another of my books, *I Loved a Paedophile*, in which I describe the stages of grooming and seduction and how easy it can be to slide into a fully abusive situation with the potential for long-lasting consequences. The story is relevant for parents who want to keep their children safe and for those who see loved ones in abusive relationships and are desperate to know how to help them escape. Most importantly, the story is relevant for anyone suffering from trauma.

The truth is, the way we've been taught to handle emotions doesn't work. Most of us have learned to manage our emotions by pushing them out of our conscious awareness. This is called denial and we do it in a variety of ways. We simply deny that we have any problems at all, we might avoid situations that trigger us, state affirmations or practice positive thinking. All of these sound like great strategies. Some of these scenarios have even become normalised by society, because we've become accustomed to believing that almost all of us are traumatised and can never recover. But here's the thing: these coping strategies can only manage the symptoms, not the underlying problem.

Like trying to pump up a tyre with a slow leak, these strategies require effort and, ultimately, they won't make your tyre roadworthy. The pain and the problems are still there. The neurons are still firing unconsciously. You're completely ignorant that you're radiating all that energy until, *Boom!* A big problem lands in your life and you can't understand where it came from. This scenario plays out all over the world: in every culture, family, boardroom, office space and relationship.

Why coping strategies don't work

If healing is possible, then why hasn't it worked for you (yet)? If you've tried to heal from the past, but have been unsuccessful, you might have been tempted to blame yourself or ask, 'What's wrong with me?' There's absolutely nothing wrong with you. You are fabulous. The reason you're still experiencing trauma from your past is simply because the techniques you've been told to use don't really work. They might work a little bit for a short while, but the problems inevitably return. What's worse is that many of these techniques can actually become part of the problem or have nasty side-effects that cause their own problems. The things that can make us feel a little better in the moment are often the same things that prevent our deep, meaningful healing.

A coping strategy is anything that helps you avoid the pain. Coping strategies attempt to treat the effect/

symptom, but fail to resolve the cause/root illness. A coping strategy masks, numbs or avoids the pain. It's superficial and any relief is limited and generally short-lived. In some situations, we need a coping strategy to get us through. (Many of us needed coping strategies to get us through the Covid-19 pandemic.) Sometimes, a coping strategy is the more practical and immediate option. For example, if you're at work, driving or giving a presentation and you suddenly have a flashback, calling up your CET practitioner or logging into the CET app on your phone to release your trauma probably isn't practical. In situations like this, you need something that will give you instant relief and allow you to cope until you can get to your practitioner or use CET.

Common coping strategies

The next section presents some common coping strategies, with the aim of identifying behaviours we might not be aware of rather than 'diagnosing' anyone or assigning blame:

- **Addictions:** Drugs, alcohol, food, shopping, video games, gambling, sex…All these things may make us feel better in the moment, but they mask the symptoms rather than treat the cause. All addictions are caused by an unmet, unconscious need. Over time, an addicted person can find themselves needing more and more 'hits' of their addiction to just feel OK, but most addictions have unpleasant, dangerous or unwanted side-effects. (Many clients have spontaneously overcome addictions after a single session of CET. One woman simply never smoked again – and she hadn't even come for smoking!)

- **Affirmations:** Affirmations also have limitations. They are useful in shifting how we feel in the moment, but they don't work to release trauma from the past by removing the block or resistance to energy. The problem isn't what we say, it's what we feel, which involves energy and emotion. To change what we feel, we need a process to release energy and emotion so that we are restored to our natural state of positivity.

- **Avoidance:** A common way of coping with trauma is to avoid anything that will trigger it. This can manifest as making every effort to avoid people, situations and circumstances that remind us of the original traumatising event or stimulus (eg, the person who's had a car accident and never drives again). It's like wearing a suicide vest, but putting the trigger switch out of sight: the vest is still there, weighing you down and it could go off at any moment. These avoidance tactics shrink our lives, making the world, and our experience of it, increasingly restricted. Life is intended to be challenging. If we feel the need to avoid a particular situation or type of environment, we limit ourselves. We deny ourselves the possibility of growth. If we are unable to rise to any and all challenges, the attempt to avoid stress becomes extremely stressful. I'm not suggesting that it's a great idea to deliberately put yourself in unpleasant situations, but if there are normal, everyday situations that you simply have to avoid because they trigger you, what you can tolerate will start to shrink, and in turn, your life will shrink. Wouldn't it be better if you had invincible emotional resilience so that you could overcome anything to achieve success?

Catharsis and 'talking about it'

You've talked about your negative feelings. You've cried. A lot. Catharsis used to be a central part of many forms of psychotherapy that, in addition to talking it out, encouraged people to hit pillows, scream, shout and cry. These activities do not release painful emotions: they *express* them. Catharsis may make us feel better temporarily or it may be a strategy for accessing energy (anger, for example, is energising), but catharsis can distract us from the root cause of the deeper issue and it doesn't remove the Source of the pain.

In fact, rather than releasing emotions, catharsis can actually reinforce them in our neurology. Every time we think a thought, feel an emotion or recall a memory, the neurons in our brain fire along the same original path.[3] This strengthens an unhelpful neurological pattern and

---

3. L Feldman Barrett, *How Emotions Are Made: The secret life of the brain* (Pan Books, 2017)

can even make things worse when small events in the present trigger past trauma.

Overanalysing

I've spoken to many people who have in-depth awareness and understanding of their problems. They know the cause and the events. They know what happened and why they feel the way they do. They understand all their patterns and triggers. They can even use their 'story' as the really good reason why their life isn't working. I've heard people tell me they want to do this or that, but then tell me they can't because of some childhood trauma or limiting belief they hold. Knowing why you have the problem and understanding it is a bit like knowing your car doesn't work because the fanbelt has broken, but not actually replacing it.

Playing the blame game

Blaming other people, organisations, society or even ourselves, for a lack of success or for negative feelings is a seductive strategy. It can attract attention and pity and leave us playing the role of the wronged victim or brave martyr. Temporarily satisfying though this might seem, it prevents us from ever healing, changing or growing. Staying in blame and resentment can also show up in unintended actions, passive-aggressive behaviours and anxiety. Avoiding taking full responsibility will always block us from achieving the success, joy and happiness we desire.

Positive thinking

Much as we'd like it to, positive thinking doesn't solve our problems. Denying the negative is not the same as removing it for good. As we will learn in the next chapter, negative emotions caused by our current situation are a sign that something isn't right. Their purpose is to tell us to take action. Positive thinking won't chase off a hungry lion, no matter how much you wish it to. Your fear, powered by adrenaline, is there to make sure you recognise the danger. Similarly, negative emotions are either telling us that something isn't right in the present, or that something wasn't right in the past, and it needs attending to. If you're in the wrong job or wrong relationship, it is completely appropriate to feel bad. That's how you know. Denying how we feel keeps us stuck in situations that we would be better off changing. When we ignore important emotional messages, they only get louder. The pain will get worse until we change something.

It can be helpful to be positive about the belief that we *can* heal and change, but realistic and honest about the presence of the problem. If you tell yourself there isn't a problem when there is, you still experience trauma and feel bad, but now you also feel bad about feeling bad and compound the problem. Our painful emotions are just information: they aren't bad or wrong. Honour them and use them to guide you to happiness. Just like that classic childhood game of 'warmer/colder', our emotions are guiding us to what we want and away from what we don't want.

Waiting for the right time

Believing we need to 'be ready' and that the way to get ready is to simply wait is really an avoidance tactic in disguise. We don't get ready by waiting. If you tell children to get ready and they carry on sitting on the sofa watching TV, they aren't getting ready. Getting ready is finding your shoes and putting them on. Getting ready to transform starts with one simple step: to decide to do it. The preliminary stages of a CET intervention are designed to get you ready quickly and easily for complete transformation.

Moving on

While each of these coping strategies may work in the short-term, they're all missing one or more of the key magic ingredients that make recovering from trauma easy with CET. Again, don't panic if you see yourself in any of these coping strategies. Remember, it's always better to know you have a problem and be working towards fixing it than to pretend everything is fine and spend the rest of your life in misery. It is my hope that by sharing my story, you will see that recovery is not only possible, but that it can be easier than you imagined.

THREE

Why Emotions?

Sitting on a cold bench, the January chill seeping through my layers of clothes, I struggle to sketch the scene before me. The progress is painful. The sketch is lifeless. Is it the cold creeping into my hands making them stiff and awkward? Even after five years of living in London, my body still hasn't acclimatised to the winter chill. I put my pencil down and stare out at the park sloping down the hill below. I wonder if I should go back to my bedsit, but that doesn't feel like home. I've only spent one night there. It's still an alien space. I've only met my housemates briefly. They seem nice, but I don't know them. I don't feel safe around them.

I realise that I am desperately lonely, but I can't think of a single person I can reach out to – no one I can pop round to see or call for a chat. I watch groups of people walking around the park, getting fresh air or watching their kids on the playground. A group of bundled-up mums with coffees huddle together, chatting and giggling, couples and gaggles of teenagers take shortcuts across the park and bands of lads kick a ball around. I feel utterly alone and lost. My mind echoes with the sound of my own thoughts:

I don't know what to do.

I don't know what to do right now.

I don't know what to do later.

I don't know what to eat for my dinner.

I don't know how to choose.

It is my first day of freedom.

I should be happy.

I should be jumping at the opportunity to everything I've dreamed of.

But where am I now?

What do I do now?

Who am I now?

Past emotions still present

After leaving Gary, I continued to live what might have looked like a normal life, but inside, I was hiding and protecting a raw, inner core of pain. I was riddled with problems and struggled in social situations. I had no idea who I was, what I liked or what I wanted. For years, my only desire had been to keep Gary happy. Beyond that, I hadn't existed.

I carved out a routine that made my life manageable. I deliberately avoided new situations, because I knew they would overwhelm me. My familiar routine was a coping strategy. I went to uni lectures and studied. I made some friends. I ate simply and rotated the same five dishes as the days turned to weeks, and weeks became months. I worked through my degree, getting solid, but not stellar, grades. I found I was good at maths. Really good. Better than many of my peers. Engineering was the perfect discipline for me. Engineering and science aren't about emotions or personality. The beam doesn't care if you love or hate it, whether it will support the load or not is based entirely on the maths. The complexity and intensity of thought that engineering required was a blessed relief from my inner emotional turmoil.

I did my best to keep a really low profile and to be quiet like Gary had trained me, but my bubbly, gregarious personality would occasionally spill out with enthusiastic outbursts. Afterwards, I'd chastise myself for being 'too this' or 'too that'. The words and voice of Gary had been programmed to run through my head after every social event. Little things fazed me, like how to order a drink or what to order if I was eating at the refectory. I was terrified of getting things wrong and being criticised for inappropriate behaviour. I was emotionally fragile and supersensitive to every word, gesture or facial expression that I could possibly interpret as a judgement. Even the slightest criticism from a friend or flatmate would trigger a cascade of hurt and shame, causing me to cry alone in my bedsit for hours. I lived life as if I had a thousand papercuts, flinching at every touch, no matter how light or gentle. Sometimes, I wished I could just disappear to make the pain stop. Burdened and crippled, I wondered what possible purpose my painful emotions could serve.

Emotions become problematic when they stop us from fulfilling our life's divine purpose by creating resistance to love. Why do we experience flashbacks, phobias, depression and despair or anxiety? Why is it when we're trying to sleep, we wake up remembering some embarrassing thing we said twenty years ago? Why do we feel nervous when we're about to speak up in a meeting, or ask a boy out on a date? These emotions seem unhelpful, so what's going on here?

It's easy for our minds to connect the past event with the emotions attached to it. Any time we experience a situation that is similar to, or reminiscent of, the original event, our unconscious mind will 'trigger' the old, unresolved emotion. Every time we feel an emotion or recall a memory, the neurons in our brain fire along the same, original path. That's why simply remembering a past situation can bring on feelings of anxiety or fear.

How does bursting into a rage because we can't open a pickle jar help us open the jar? Why can one apparently insignificant comment destroy our confidence and cause us to hit the bottle or biscuit tin to numb our emotional pain? Why do grief and heartbreak consume us, sometimes for years at a time?

On the origin of our species' feelings

The human experience of emotions is universal, but scientists, biologists, psychologists and neuroscientists have so far been unable to agree upon a standard definition for them. We *do* know that emotions are linked to our survival and how we experience life. Emotions affect everything. They drive us forward or hold us back. Without emotions, life would not only be dull, but meaningless.

Historically, our emotions served an evolutionary and biological purpose.[4] For a moment, imagine our human

---

4. DM Buss, *Evolutionary Psychology: The new science of the mind*, 6th edition (Routledge, 2019)

existence in prehistoric times. Humans evolved from hunter-gatherers living in small tribal groups. Finding food was a full-time job and our emotions were often responses to survival scenarios. Imagine walking out to gather food and coming across a large bush covered in delicious, ripe berries. How would you feel? Probably some mixture of 'positive' feelings – excitement, relief, anticipation or joy. Perhaps you are part of a group of hunters and you've just spotted a herd of tasty beasts. You might also feel excitement, joy or anticipation. If a snake then chases you away from your bush of tasty delights or your hunt is unsuccessful, you might return to your hut feeling anxious, disappointed, frustrated or angry.

Now imagine that just as you are reaching out your hand to collect some of those yummy fruits or spear a gazelle, you spot a hungry lion not far in the distance. Flooded with adrenaline, you feel *fear*, which is entirely appropriate. Fear keeps us safe and alive. Fear prompts your body to take action by removing you from danger or neutralising the threat (think 'fight or flight'). After escaping the jaws of the lion, you'll remember the frightening situation, but, if your emotional response is working appropriately, you won't feel the fear.

Perhaps as you're making your escape from that hungry lion, you trip and twist your ankle. Ouch – that hurt! Physical pain lets us know we've been injured and keeps us from further harming ourselves. Pain also helps keep us still while we are healing. The pain stops once we are no longer in danger and our wounds have healed. Once your physical body has healed, you'll remember that it was a painful experience, but you won't feel the actual pain.

Consider childbirth. People who have experienced childbirth can remember the hours of agony, but they no longer experience the physical pain. Why? It would serve no purpose for us to feel pain when the cause of the pain has been removed. That's exactly how our emotions *should* work. Once we are out of the unpleasant situation, we should be able to remember that we felt painful emotions, but we should not actually feel them.

But early human emotions weren't entirely reactions to simply surviving. Humans experienced more complex emotions too, sometimes called 'higher emotions.' Our higher emotions also served an evolutionary purpose. Bonds of connection and kinship encourage us to support each other so that the group can survive and thrive. Love, for example, is a powerful way to inspire connection to the family or tribe. The presence of such emotions greatly increases the success of the group as a whole and of each individual within the group.

Conversely, emotions such as guilt, shame and remorse prevent an individual from behaving in ways that might damage the safety of the tribe. These emotions encourage individuals to help each other, increasing the evolutionary success of the group. Imagine Kral sneaking into the food hut late one night and raiding the stores of meat in a midnight binge that ultimately makes him sick. When the rest of tribe discovers what he's done, they give him a right telling off. Not only has Kral wasted the efforts of the hunters, but he's also jeopardised the tribe's ability to make it through the winter with enough food. Ashamed of his greed and poor choices, Kral feels guilty and vows never to steal from the food cache again. This is why fear of rejection from our tribal group is so strong. Without the connection, mutual support and strength of the group, we could literally die. Hence, we want to be loved, accepted and connected to our group. Emotions are not only useful, but they are also vital to our survival.

Millennia later, we experience the same emotions as our distant ancestors, but in different contexts. These days, we are rarely in the type of life-threatening situations that might have provoked fear in our ancestors. Outside of some specific circumstances, most of us are more likely to find ourselves in *livelihood*-threatening situations. We might fear losing our job or we might fear the end of an important relationship (especially if we are financially interconnected with our partner). Even if these situations don't threaten us physically, the implications for our personal success and happiness are clear.

Like our early ancestors, when working appropriately, emotions give us feedback. Much like the 'warmer/colder' game, some emotions tell us we are moving away from what we desire, while others show us that we are moving towards our goals. It's normal for us to want to categorise our emotions and so we often label those 'colder' emotions – the ones that tell us we are moving away from our goals – as 'negative emotions'. In CET, we sort all the 'negative' emotions that we feel into six categories: anger, sadness, fear, hurt, guilt and shame. (I will explain why these six emotions are important later, but for now, what's important is that we feel something and it doesn't feel good.)

Nothing either good or bad, but thinking makes it so[5]

Shakespeare was a great psychologist. In one of his plays, Hamlet, the main character, rightly objects to our human tendency to slap morality labels onto things that do not require our judgement. Take emotions, for example. Our emotions have long been portrayed as problems that need to be solved, avoided or shoved under the rug. Western society has conditioned us to suppress our emotions. Men do so because society tells them that expressing emotions is not 'manly' and women fear being perceived as 'emotional', 'hysterical' or 'too sensitive'. We've labelled certain emotional responses as illogical and irrational and then used such judgements to reinforce biased stereotypes.

---

5. Part of quote from Shakespeare's play, *Hamlet*

As if a general societal disdain for emotions isn't tough enough, we also tend to separate our emotions into two categories and label them accordingly: positive or negative. Most of us agree that joy, love, excitement and gratitude, for example, feel good and are 'positive', while sadness, anger, hurt, guilt and fear, for example, feel bad and are 'negative'. The problem with phrases like 'good and bad' and 'positive and negative' is that they come with baggage. When we label something good and another thing bad, we are implicitly making a moral judgement. Good things are 'right' (ie, what we *should* feel) and bad things are 'wrong' (ie, what we *shouldn't* feel).

The truth is that emotions are neither good nor bad, positive nor negative. Emotions are simply emotions. Depending on their context, some emotions can help us and some can hinder us. In some cases, emotions are appropriate and useful. At other times, our emotions may be inappropriate and may not be serving us. All emotions are useful as a feedback mechanism to let us know if we are moving towards ('getting warmer') or away from ('colder') our goals and dreams and even our life's purpose. Positive feedback from our boss after a presentation? Our subsequent sense of pride and satisfaction tells us that we are on the right track. Negative feedback? Our shame and embarrassment tell us something's not quite right. That's clear enough. It's easy to understand this emotional logic in real time.

The Big Bang Theory: our emotional response cycle

No matter how incomprehensible our emotional responses may seem, there *is* a divine logic to them. Our emotions give us the information we need to identify and heal from trauma by providing feedback. Understanding this process is an important step in recovering from trauma. This is the process I call the ERC. When the ERC runs properly, we experience an appropriate emotional response and take appropriate action. The experience has taught us something and that knowledge empowers us. If the ERC malfunctions or gets stuck for some reason, we can find ourselves in trouble.

Imagine you are walking down your local high street. Suddenly, you hear a loud bang. You look around, trying to understand the situation. If you're in North America or are prone to watching lots of action movies, you might think, 'Gunshot!' and drop to the pavement or run for cover. Or, you might notice that workers at a building site nearby have just thrown a large, heavy object into a skip below. You feel momentarily startled, but your heart rate settles and you continue with your errands.

Congratulations. You have successfully cycled through all four stages of the ERC. What we describe as an 'emotion' or 'feeling' is actually only one part of an advanced neurological process. When our ERC is running smoothly, it moves swiftly through four phases and produces resolution and learning.

Stimulus (something happens) – We experi-
ent that requires us to change our behaviour
towards our goals or avoid setbacks. This
event could be huge and tragic, or seemingly small
and insignificant.

Phase 2: Thought (we think about what happened) –
Consciously or unconsciously, our mind attempts make
sense of the event(s) to generate an appropriate response. When we apply appropriate meaning to the
event, we learn to adapt how we think about what happened or how we behave.

**Phase 3: Feeling (we experience a physiological re-
sponse)** – For example, fear causes our heart to beat
faster, our muscles to tense and hands to sweat. Specific facial expressions are a common physiological response.

Phase 4: Action (we do/stop doing something) –
Finally, we have a behavioural response. We take an
action or stop taking an action to achieve our goals. If
we act, but don't get the result we're looking for, ideally
the cycle should just re-start and continue until we do
get the desired result. When our thoughts and actions
correspond and we achieve our desired outcomes, we
feel good.

Our ERC in action

Imagine you see a large animal (stimulus). 'That looks big and dangerous,' you think to yourself, perhaps outside of your conscious awareness (thought). Your heart races, your breath quickens and you feel fear (emotion). Then you slowly back away, hide in a convenient bush, or run like heck (action).

If you can't imagine running into a large and scary beast, try this modern equivalent: As you walk past your boss's office, she shouts your name and calls you over (stimulus). 'Uh-oh, she sounds angry. Did I mess up?' Then you realise you forgot to attach a report to an email (thought). You feel anxious and guilty (emotion). You immediately go into her office to explain and resend the email – with the attachment this time (action).

What happens after the cycle completes is crucial. The purpose of the ERC is to teach us which thoughts and actions bring us closer to our goals, and which do not. After completing a cycle, we should be able to appropriately understand and interpret what has happened. Ideally, if our actions and thoughts are aligned and have brought us closer to our goal, our mind stores this process as a memorised strategy or behavioural pattern. For now, we will call this 'learnings'.

Learnings can be simple and straightforward, or they can be more abstract. In the example above, the learnings might be as simple as: 'I will make sure to pay attention when sending work emails in the future. I have a good memory and will use it.' The key thing about learnings is that they are always empowering: they relate to you personally and they are useful for the future, but what if:

- The stimulus is too great?

- We can't comprehend the experience or find meaning?

- Our feelings are disallowed?

- We aren't able to respond in an effective way?

We will be stuck and unable to progress to the next phase. Our minds will keep continuously looping around the cycle in our memory, attempting to gain resolution. That is why we feel painful emotions in the present even when their origins lie in events that are long past. A non-functioning ERC is the definition of trauma.

When our ERC attempts to complete but is prevented, a block – a resistance to love energy – is created. As we will discuss in detail later on, even a relatively minor amount of resistance in the ERC can build up over time, snowballing into greater and more significant, painful experiences. In fact, a malfunctioning ERC is the reason why the coping strategies we mentioned earlier aren't working for you. Coping strategies do not address the origin of our pain and cannot fully repair a non-functioning ERC. Only CET can target the original malfunction in our ERC, repair it, release all the built-up resistance, rebalance our energy flow, create new neural pathways that increase the free flow of love energy and deeply, and profoundly, reconnect us to Source.

FOUR
Why The Past Haunts Us

It's around 2002. My toddler daughter is delighting in a new hat and pushing it onto my head. Every time she pushes it down, I can't bear it. I pull it off. I do it gently and try to explain that mummy doesn't want to wear the hat. My husband chides me, 'Just wear the hat, she wants to play.' He grabs the hat and tries to pull it onto my head. Suddenly, I start to panic. I'm terrified. My emotions flip into irritation and then anger. I don't want to wear the hat. I snap, more sharply than I want to, or the situation demands. Now I've upset everyone, and I don't even know why.

I'm discussing what happened with my husband and apologising for snapping and suddenly: *Bam!* I am back in the flat with Gary. He holds his hand to my head, forcing my face to the wall. When he did this, I couldn't see him. I couldn't see anything. I felt vulnerable. I panicked. This was a common occurrence and one of his petty power-plays. He didn't actually physically harm me, he just restrained me, but years later, when people applied pressure on my head (even when it was in kind, gentle or playful ways), the touch triggered the memory of my past trauma.

When events in the present remind us of our traumatic past, even when we are safe and we know nothing bad is going to happen, we call this a 'trigger'. When something happens in the present that, consciously or unconsciously, recalls past trauma, we re-experience the same emotions we felt during the traumatic event, resulting in an inappropriate response. Being triggered is a common human reaction to unresolved pain. There is nothing 'wrong' with you for experiencing a trigger. It simply means that the ERC wasn't completed. The ERC can get stuck or fail along the way in any one of the four phases: stimulus, thought, feeling or action. The brilliant thing about CET is that we can use it to repair any, and all, of these possible situations.

Phase One: Stimulus size doesn't matter

Many people imagine that a traumatic experience must be one big, horrible event – something tragic, immense and significant, but that's not necessarily the case. When it comes to stimuli that lead to trauma, it's not the size of the event or experience that matters.

SNOWBALLING

It's mid-2020. The Covid-19 pandemic has confined us all at home. Eleanor is on a Zoom call with a client, going through the finer points of the legal defence for her client's divorce. The client is stressed about the hearing. It is Eleanor's job to stay calm and construct the case to get the best outcome. It's detailed and nuanced and requires a lot of thinking.

From somewhere else in the house, Eleanor hears the voices of her two children. They are doing their schoolwork (or are supposed to be). She has tried to set them up on their iPads, helped them log into their various classrooms, and tried to understand (and then explain) lessons and concepts she hasn't used for years. Eleanor tries to ignore the noise.

Her client continues to be upset. Legal cases are often stressful, even when the client is one of the good guys. Eleanor still has to provide a decent defence and uphold her reputation and nickname as 'the rottweiler' because of her ability to fight ruthlessly for her clients (despite her veneer of 'niceness').

The noise from the other room rises in volume and intensity and becomes laden with emotions. She hears her two children squabbling – *again*. Eleanor can't ignore them any longer. She snaps. She ends the call with her client, storms into the other room and lets rip. Every bit of frustration, exhaustion and anger comes out. She yells, and yells and yells. The kids stop and stare in stunned silence.

This is what happens when multiple stimuli snowball into one, traumatic experience. It's not that any single element is too intense. Eleanor could've dealt with each situation individually, but juggling work, clients, her team, parenting, schooling, partnering and house management in difficult and ever-changing circumstances and with the underlying threats of economic uncertainty and health worries about contracting Covid-19... Suddenly, it had all been too much. Several factors influence how traumatic any given stimulus can be:

- Intensity

- Rate of change

- Duration

- Repetition

All four of them, working together or separately, influence how we experience and interpret any given stimulus. Combined in the right (or should that be wrong) way, they will push our nervous system over our inner threshold level. A common misconception about trauma is that it's the intensity of the emotion or what happened during the event itself that makes something traumatic, but it's really how all these factors combine to create our experience of the stimulus. Many people assume their past isn't traumatic because the event wasn't dramatic, yet little daily struggles can build up to create and install trauma in our neurology. We all have a threshold of what we can deal with. If the combined stimuli of our life's current situation are below our threshold level, we feel fine and we can cope. If the rate of change, intensity, duration and repetition overstimulate our nervous system beyond our threshold of endurance, we feel as if we cannot cope. This prevents our ERC from completing.

Intensity

As the name suggests, intensity refers to how intensely we experience a particular event. Intensity depends on each person's unique neurology. A simple example is the scary scale. On a scale from someone jumping out and saying 'Boo,' to being held at knifepoint, one is clearly more intense than the other.

Rate of change

How quickly do we go from a calm, relaxed state, to a heightened state? We experience a fast rate of change when, for example, a sudden, loud noise startles us out of our Poldark daydream. Being abruptly brought back to reality isn't likely to cause trauma, but it illustrates the point. Our nervous system takes time to adapt to new stimuli. The rate of change is a function of both the difference between the calm (pre-stimulus) state and the heightened emotional state (post–stimulus), and the time for the change to take place.

OUT OF THE BLUE

On the morning of 11 September 2001, Jenn was getting ready for the first day of classes of her final year at uni. She had a job interview lined up that morning, work on her honours thesis to get started on and friends to catch up with. She was excited and looking forward to it all. One minute she was in the shower, and the next, the walls of her apartment were shaking ominously. One minute she was putting on her best 'I'm a responsible adult' interview suit, and the next, she was standing outside looking up her smoke-filled street and surrounded by people running in all directions. Shouts, cries and white ash filled the air. A few blocks away, the World Trade Centre was ablaze.

Adrenalin coursed around her body, and she felt fear, confusion and a number of other intense emotions. Such a sudden change in circumstances caused Jenn's nervous system to go from a state of low arousal (feeling relaxed, calm or steady) to a state of high arousal and emotion in a short time. Jenn was suddenly in a state of shock.

When we can't manage this rapid emotional change of state, we often describe this as shock. The more quickly the shift from calm relaxation to high alertness, the greater the rate of change of the state. High rates of change will put more stress on the nervous system than slow changes will and can lead to long-term resistances being installed.

Repetition

How many times do we experience an event (or similar events)? Abuse is a classic example of repetition.
People who have experienced abusive relationships
often struggle to pinpoint one particular event that was
horrific or challenging. Instead, it's the slow and steady
drip, drip, drip of negativity and criticism that builds
up over time. Like a thousand papercuts that leave you
feeling raw and sore, abusive situations will slowly,
but surely, take their toll on your emotional wellbeing.
Over time, these situations are likely to create limiting
beliefs. People who experience abuse often begin to
believe they must in some way deserve this poor treatment. Self-blame explains how our mind rationalises
long-term, low-level abuse and mistreatment.

Duration

How long did the event last? Did the crisis situation
only last for a few seconds or minutes, or was it hours
or even days? Duration refers to the length of time we
are exposed to the stimulus. Whenever our nervous
system is exposed to that stimulus, the ERC will be
running, and we will be feeling the emotion.

Phase Two: Thought – what does it all mean?

James came to me suffering with PTSD after being involved in a freak accident. His car hit a twelve-year-old girl on a bike and she died. He felt terrible, even though he knew, logically, that it was just a terrible accident and everyone around him (including the girl's parents) assured him that he'd done nothing wrong. The event played over in his mind repeatedly. Counselling and traditional therapies had failed to take away his flashbacks.

It was just one of those tragic things that happen randomly. That was the problem. When an event is truly random or meaningless, it is much more likely to be traumatic than an event or situation that we can make some sense of. With no reason or apparent cause for this tragedy that had cut a life short, how could he resolve it in his mind? At a loss to understand what meaning or larger purpose his accident might have served, James's ERC was stuck and he suffered from flashbacks – a symptom of PTSD.

Flashbacks happen when we experience a stimulus in the present that reminds us of a past event. The stimulus triggers the ERC to run, but it can't complete because the cycle is damaged or blocked. James was having flashbacks because the ERC hadn't fully completed. It was stuck in the second phase – thought – where we try to make sense of what's happening and find a greater meaning. In James's case, because the event *made no sense*, he couldn't apply appropriate meaning (thought). When this happens, emotional energy gets stuck in our nervous system, creating a boundary in our neurology. The mind continues to replay the memory, attempting to complete the cycle and apply meaning to what happened, until it can successfully complete the cycle. Without some kind of intervention, the individual will never complete the cycle fully or successfully. This is what happens to someone experiencing PTSD. This is how trauma is stored in the nervous system.

This is where James was when he came to me for help. During our CET work together, the CET process led James to discover a new and appropriate meaning to the event and to make sense of the past experience in a way that allowed the ERC to complete. (We'll cover how CET works in more depth in a later chapter.) At the moment when the repair to his ERC happened, James went quiet. I could feel something happening for him. His eyes closed, but they moved rapidly beneath his eyelids. His breathing sped up and then slowed, and his entire body relaxed as he began to weep – not the anguished weeping of distress, but the gentle weeping of redemption and forgiveness. It was like watching a spiritual awakening before my eyes.

When we'd finished the process, he asked if he could share what he'd experienced. 'It was extraordinary,' he said. 'I saw her, and she seemed to speak to me. She said that this is what she wanted. What she'd come for. She had another life to go and live. Now that she'd experienced what she wanted from this one, it was time for her to move on. She told me that it was what she wanted, and what her parents wanted, too. I don't understand it. I don't know exactly how this all fits together, but it feels right. It makes some sense now.'

We have no way of ever knowing if James's vision was 'true' or 'accurate'. It's entirely possible that his unconscious mind constructed the experience to find meaning in a tragic situation. Whether or not this is the truth isn't the point. The point is that once his mind had found meaning, the emotional trauma was released, and James could go on to live a happy life.

WHAT'S THE POINT?

Sitting in my therapy chair picking his fingernails, Adam, a marine, reeled off his list of symptoms: feeling anxious, worrying about everything, depression, irritability, inability to tolerate loud noises, and lack of motivation, so he didn't do the things he needed to and then felt guilt, shame and anxiety. He couldn't sleep, and when he did, he had nightmares. These were the classic symptoms of PTSD.

PTSD isn't really much different to any other kind of trauma, there's just more of it. We applied what was fast becoming my standard protocol for this. I recommended some exercises to calm his nervous system – only simple coping strategies, but they gave almost instant relief to some of the worst effects. This allowed us to find the cause of the trauma. Tearfully, he described his event: the truck carrying one of his mates had hit a landmine, seriously injuring him. Adam stayed with his friend, keeping him calm and administering lifesaving first aid until the medical evacuation arrived. His friend had suffered head injuries that changed his personality forever. This event took Adam over his threshold. With his nervous system in overload, he lost the meaning or point to it all. Suddenly, nothing was worth this. His friend was alive, but no longer the same person.

Adam's guilt that it hadn't been him was compounded with shame when he realised that had he not been joshing with his friend, their commander wouldn't have split the pair up and put them in separate trucks. Had he not been acting the fool he would have also been in that truck. He would have also likely been injured or killed. He was deeply relieved, but so ashamed of thinking and feeling this way. This stopped his ERC from running and put him in trauma.

During the CET release process, he accessed a new perspective. Adam experienced connecting with the 'Higher Self' of his best friend, who told him, 'You're a good man. Keep being a good man. There's more good for you to do.' In a follow-up session, Adam described how he was retraining and going to teach in primary schools. He spoke enthusiastically about the anti-bullying work he wanted to do, teaching boys how to be good men.

Adam was just one example of the CET work I undertook with marines suffering from PTSD on returning from combat zones. The soldiers would often describe how confident they felt at the beginning of their tours, secure in the knowledge that they were fighting for something worthwhile. They would risk life and limb because they believed their sacrifice served a just purpose. Added to that, the closeness of the friendship of those in the services made their experiences bearable.

The marines who experienced PTSD all had a similar experience. At some point, either in an instant or over the course of time, they realised that the war, the battles, the death, the pain and the risk had lost their meaning. At this point, they had trouble serving and began having symptoms of PTSD. CET helped them to identify another, higher, meaning to wartime trauma. Each marine found a unique higher meaning – be it the realisation of their inherent goodness; that they were worthy, strong and loved; an understanding of the degree to which they had been tested and risen to the challenge; the discovery that their experience had contributed to some greater purpose or the recognition of something related to their specific circumstances. With a new, empowering and expansive meaning, they were able to release their pain and recover from their traumatic experiences.

The meaning-making fuel powering our reality engines

Our mind craves meaning. Without a readily available meaning, our mind will invent one, even if it's negative, limiting or nonsensical. We call these negative meanings 'limiting beliefs'. Beliefs are convictions that we hold to be true. They are stored in our unconscious mind and influence what we create in our reality. Limiting beliefs are usually installed when our mind tries to make meaning out of traumatic or painful events in our past. They take the form of negative or restricting stories we tell about ourselves, and they come with baggage in the form of negative emotions.

Many of us can trace our limiting beliefs back to a single event in our childhood, before the age of seven (this is something we get into during CET sessions). Some examples of limiting beliefs include:

- I'm not good enough.

- I'm not worthy.

- I'm a bad person.

- I can't...

FROM WRONG CALL TO LIMITING BELIEF

At a meeting with the whole company, June's boss called on her to provide some information. She wasn't prepared for this request and, put on the spot, she pulled her best guess from her memory rather than asking for time to gather the correct data. Her boss wrote down her response and the team continued work on the project using Jane's data. It quickly became apparent that something wasn't right. The team double-checked June's information and confirmed that her data had been incorrect. June felt humiliated. In a properly functioning ERC, June would have learned from this event and simply used the experience as a lesson in the importance of asking for more time instead of spouting out knee-jerk answers. Unfortunately, June's mind installed a limiting belief instead: in her unconscious mind, June interpreted her mistake as a sign that she was stupid.

This unconscious, limiting belief continued to impact her negatively for many years. It caused her to doubt everything; she battled to make any decisions; she didn't ask for promotions and constantly blamed and berated herself. She would always assume she was wrong when challenged – even if she was right. Her self-doubt was affecting everything: her work, her career, her income and her relationships. Even her family would make jokes about how stupid she was. That's how any belief we hold about ourselves that limits or diminishes us will cause the ERC to become stuck.

Why didn't June realise that committing one mistake didn't make her a dummy for life? Why couldn't she just let it go? Some limiting beliefs are easy to spot. We even say them out loud, sometimes as throwaway comments. Others can be challenging. Identifying them takes practice and skill, because they have been installed in our unconscious mind and are mostly beyond awareness. Even if we logically and consciously know that something cannot be so, the unconscious belief will still be held as the truth. That's why we often have no idea why we feel the way we feel and behave the way we do. Our ERC is stuck on a limiting belief and can't complete the cycle. The limiting belief is blocking the smooth flow of love energy and that's why we might feel 'stuck'. We keep feeling the same, shitty feelings and experience a pattern of repeating behaviour that doesn't serve our Higher Self. If you are not healing despite your best efforts and intentions, it's likely that the culprit is an unconscious limiting belief.

When June and I worked together, we were able to unearth her unconscious limiting belief and release it. June wasn't stupid: she just *thought* she was. Once we identified the limiting belief clogging June's ERC and released it, she began to trust her own knowledge and her ability to gather data and information. She went on to gain a promotion and a raise. Her husband and family began to respect her more and she felt loved, too.

Beliefs or reality: what's the difference?

People often dismiss the idea that our beliefs are behind the reality we experience. I often hear clients object, 'This isn't a "belief", it's *real*'. They aren't wrong – real things are real, but real situations and experiences can be created by our beliefs.

Having no money in your bank account is certainly real, but we know that making money happens when we take certain actions and don't take others; and taking (or not taking) those actions can be easier or harder depending on the beliefs we hold. If you believe you are unworthy or don't deserve to be rich, you are less likely to go for a promotion or ask for a big sale. Even if you do pursue advancement, you might unconsciously self-sabotage your success. As a result, you don't make the money you want. You might also take actions that result in you having less money. For example, you might go on a shopping spree to make yourself feel better for not getting the raise/promotion/job you were aiming for. This is how we can understand the reality of 'having no money': as an experience caused by one or more limiting beliefs. Remember, many limiting beliefs are completely out of our awareness, so we don't even know they are there. All we see are the results.

CET identifies and zaps limiting beliefs, freeing up the blocks in your ERC so that your emotions can run smoothly again and you can experience the free flow of love energy. In the meantime, the take-away is that it's not necessarily the traumatic event or situation that's the problem – it's what we unconsciously make it mean. What makes it possible for humans to endure what seems to be unendurable is that it has meaning, but what about situations that have lost their meaning?

Phase Three: Feeling all the feels

Even if we are able to understand the meaning of an event, our emotional response can get stuck in the third phase of the cycle: feeling. Ideally, we will move through this stage smoothly. We feel our emotion, take appropriate action and change the situation to get the outcome we desire. However, culture and society have a lot to answer for here.

There are spoken and unspoken rules about emotions – who can feel what, and when. An obvious example is how girls and boys are socialised differently. Girls are usually discouraged from showing anger. They're told it's not ladylike to speak loudly, shout, be aggressive or even assertive. They face labels such as 'hysterical', 'emotional', 'shrill', 'strident' and even 'bitch'. Likewise, boys are discouraged from showing their love, compassion, fear or hurt. 'Big boys don't cry,' and men may be labelled 'sissy', 'weak' or 'gay' for openly demonstrating emotions that haven't been socially coded as manly. Our culture is making inroads with gender roles and expectations, but not enough. The effects of limiting socialisation are still apparent in the vast array of limiting beliefs we carry about what emotions we *should* or *should not* feel.

In these situations, when we are faced with an internalised rule or limiting belief about our emotions, our ERC gets stuck. When we prevent ourselves from feeling and validating those emotions and then moving on to take action, we might keep returning to phase two to try and find another meaning for our emotions. A girl might believe she was wrong to feel angry about whatever injustice she rightfully identified; a boy might believe it was a sign of weakness to feel love or compassion. This is how limiting beliefs and dysfunctional behavioural patterns are installed.

Phase Four: Action – Fight, flight, or f*** it

Finally, our ERC can break down in the fourth phase, when we fail to act, or we *do* act, but things don't go the way we thought they would...In our modern lives we often face situations that lead to fear, but most of us rarely need to physically fight or flee from anything or anyone. We may experience the fear of losing a job, not getting a job, getting sick, going broke, etc. In general, instead of fighting or fleeing, we need to stay calm, think, plan and use accurate judgement to act in ways that get us the results we want. We need to find ways to release our fear or channel it appropriately.

If we act, but we don't have certain skills or abilities, our actions might not get us the desired result. For example, a hunter facing down a hungry lion might throw a spear and miss. The hungry lion is still there and the risk of death or injury is still real. Ideally, after narrowly escaping the lion's clutches, our hunter would go through the ERC, find the meaning (practice spear throwing more) and follow up with diligent practice. Now more skilled with the spear, our hunter is less likely to miss next time, so this scary event has led to a better outcome in the long-term.

Sadly, this situation could also go another way. After his narrow escape, he might go through the ERC but install a limiting belief: 'I'm a lousy hunter and a big disappointment to my tribe,' which would lead to a downward spiral.

The good news is that we don't have to experience downward spirals, and if we do, we can recover. CET makes it possible for us to release limiting beliefs and other inappropriate meanings so our ERC can run smoothly and install an empowering strategy for the future. When you learn how to use CET, you'll have bad experiences (CET can't make us superhuman), but you'll be able to handle emotional pain from the past, rise above it, overcome it and still experience the exquisite joy of – well – living!

FIVE

The Road To Recovery

If you'd been with me on that icy November day, you would have seen me leave the shabby, poorly lit office of a small manufacturing business in north London. My boss had hauled me over the coals, blaming me for problems he couldn't control. I hated my job and my bully of a boss. Every day was something to simply get through until I could surrender to sleep. I craved change. I didn't want to settle for 'good enough', but I didn't know how or where to start. The only thing that gave me any joy was riding my bicycle. I was training, hoping to get good enough to be accepted into a professional cycling team. It could be the escape from the shit-hole that was my life.

The frost was already forming on the ground as I changed into my cycling gear. I stood for a moment at the door, deciding between my woolly hat or my helmet. I don't know what it was that made me do it, but I actually took off my hat to put on my helmet. Had I not worn my helmet that day, things would be different.

It was a ten-mile route. I was coming up a slight incline to one of the final roundabouts. I looked right and saw it was clear. Then, out the corner of my eye I saw something. It was a white car. I looked at the driver. He was looking straight ahead. I knew he hadn't seen me. I got a jolt of adrenaline. '*Look!*' I shouted. He didn't. I had to make a split-second decision. I could brake so that I wouldn't hit him, but I knew how fast I was going and I'd end up slamming into the side of him. Or, I could speed up and try to get ahead of him. I pedalled fast and hard. I almost made it, but for 2 inches (5 cm), I would have cleared the bonnet.

I was thrown high into the air. I landed on my right, breaking most of the bones on that side of my body. The next thing I knew, I was floating, looking down at my body. My elbow was bent at a crazy angle. I felt a presence beside me, and it gave me a choice. 'You can come with me, or you can go back. It's up to you.' I chose to live. More than that, I made the conscious decision to finally, and fully, release myself from the pain and trauma I was carrying. I was going to figure out how to make life work.

Back to basics

As soon as I had recovered enough from what I later came to refer to as my 'near-death experience', I set out to find out how I could free myself from my emotional pain and live a joy-filled life. The entire topic was new to me, but I was an engineer and a researcher. One thing engineers know is how to take things apart to figure out how they work. I understood the scientific method and I was always on the lookout for patterns. Patterns give us clues to the rules that govern our world. Now, I was looking for the rules of life. I treated my commitment to a better, fully functional life as a research project and made myself the test subject.

I tried lots of stuff. Some of it worked; some of it didn't. Some of it worked a little. After decades of slogging through every kind of healing modality out there, this long journey brought me back to basics – something we scientists call 'first principles'. When we're stretching the bounds of what we know, we have to start what with we know. We go back to the bedrock, where we can be certain, and build from there. When I went back to what I was certain of, I realised a simple truth. All of the healing modalities that I was familiar with could be sorted into two categories: those that approached releasing emotions psychologically, and those that approached releasing emotions spiritually.

Dam these painful emotions

Imagine our nervous system as a vast network of energy channels, similar to a network of flexible pipes, through which water flows. For our purposes, the water represents love energy (information or thoughts). In a well-functioning system, the water flows freely, without impediments or blockages. When our ERC is blocked, we experience a disruption to the free flow of love energy. When love energy hits resistance, that resistance acts like a dam – the 'upstream' side becomes congested or flooded. The 'downstream' side empties out, with only a trickle of energy flowing. It's not the resistance itself that's the problem – it's the difference in energy levels on either side of the resistance.

Both psychological and spiritual therapies attempt to address the problem of 'blocked' or 'clogged' neurological/spiritual pathways. Each set of approaches works in some ways and fails in others. Let's take a closer look at them.

Psychological/neurological therapies

In general, psychological- or neurological-based therapies seek to understand and analyse. They tend towards diagnosis, labelling, classifying and exploring events, and providing alternative strategies to change behaviour. This approach seeks to make sense of both the external events and the internal experience, and your response to it. For example, you go to your therapist and examine what's troubling you. After some time, you understand what happened and how and why you feel the way you do/did. You might even change some patterns and strategies.

Returning to our model of flows and blockages, we can say that psychological/neurological therapies aim to create *new* channels and pathways that bypass the block or resistance, or they may actually remove the resistance. Of course, some therapies go deeper than others, and this approach has demonstrable merit, but it doesn't rebalance the energy in the channel.

Think of a traffic jam. Just because the wreck has been removed doesn't necessarily mean the traffic disappears. It takes some time to return to a steady flow. The same is true in our energetic system. Even after a resistance has been removed, the downstream side is still depleted, and the upstream side still congested. It may slowly rebalance, but this process can take a long time. In addition, because we still feel the painful emotion every time we think about the problem or experience a triggering event, we not only feel the pain of the imbalance, but the unresolved congestion also acts like a new block. That's why talking therapies and psychoanalysis often use the phrase 'work on your problem' or 'process emotions'. They are referring to the process of rebalancing the energy imbalance. Neurological/psychological processes can work, but they have their limitations.

Spiritually based approaches

Spiritually based approaches, on the other hand, aim to rebalance energy levels symbolically. Rather than attempting to understand, evaluate or even uncover the events from the past, they direct attention to addressing instances of energetic imbalances. Energy healers use one of many energetic techniques (eg, Reiki, Theta-Healing®, Quantum healing), and seek to rebalance energy. Indeed, many use the term 'energy balancing' in their descriptions. The healer will replenish the 'downstream' side and may also discharge some of the excess energy on the 'upstream' side. We have a balancing session and, yes, we feel great. The love energy is now equalised on either side of the block. The spiritual or energy healing has acted like a pump, shifting the water from behind the dam to the area downstream.

But even the best Reiki session can't remove the Source or cause of the imbalance. The block is still there. Over time, the energy will become imbalanced again. Unless you treat the cause of the imbalance, you can count on experiencing that painful emotion again. You might start asking yourself, 'Why me? Not this again?' You may experience the same painful emotions, even if the situation is different. You might return to your energy healer for more sessions and, once again, feel great. Indeed, some forms of energy healing actually suggest you see them weekly for at least six weeks for 'top-ups'. Energy healing works, but not permanently.

How I learned to 'reCET'

Both the approaches described above work – a bit. Neither approach works fully, or permanently. My 'aha' moment came when I realised that to create a complete *and* permanent change, we need both. I used this insight to develop an entirely new healing process that lives at the intersection of psychological and spiritual healing: psycho-spiritual healing. That's how CET was born.

The real power and effectiveness of CET is that it clears the block *and* floods the neurological pathways with energy to flush your system and completely rebalance it. CET literally resets your system to how it was before the block. In the next few pages, I'll share with you my personal experiences with a range of different healing therapies and how each of them brought me one step closer to formulating CET. Every experience, every new method, all the new knowledge I gained brought me to where I needed to be to synthesise everything I knew. By following me on my journey and seeing through my eyes what worked (and what didn't), you'll have a better understanding of what makes CET different from other healing modalities.

I should stress again that these are my personal impressions of all these techniques. My aim is to present my own responses to the experiences I had, not to pass judgement on all practitioners of these therapies.

Psychoanalysis

I got a referral to a psychoanalyst from a professional association whose members were considered well-qualified and skilled.

I was to meet the therapist at his house, which made me uncomfortable. Social settings were problematic for me and visiting his house, albeit in a professional capacity, added an extra layer of uncertainty. In our first session, he explained the fee structure and how the therapy was intended to work. I was expected to see him three times a week for fifty-minute sessions, during which time I was to talk about whatever was on my mind. Talking, he said, would help me to 'find the answer within'. He explained that he would hardly speak at all. I could hope for some sort of resolution, transformation or change after three to five years. (This would mean a considerable financial commitment on my part, but I wanted to heal, so I thought I should try it.)

During my first session, I sat in an armchair facing him while he explained that during our next session I would be lying down on the couch. The 'couch' was actually a single bed, positioned so that I couldn't see the therapist. The idea was that I would be able to speak freely if I couldn't see him. At his encouragement, during the next session, I lay on his couch. Or rather, I tried to. Almost as soon as my head touched the bed, I panicked. A jolt of adrenaline shot through me. I lay still, listening to every movement he made. I had gotten through five years with an unpredictable man by staying alert and watching him. I survived by paying attention. Lying on my therapist's couch, I didn't feel relaxed. I felt unsafe. I couldn't see the therapist. I couldn't move quickly from a prone position. Through sheer force of will I made myself stay there until the session ended.

I didn't go back. Psychoanalysis was not going to work for me. Its main premise is that retelling painful events from the past leads to greater understanding of the event, which eventually heals the problem. It might, but it also might not. Psychoanalysis is an attempt at finding meaning (Phase Two in the ERC). It might eventually do this, but I don't see it as particularly efficient or reliable. In addition, retelling and reliving my past, as well as the situation itself, triggered my emotional pain. It wasn't the first and wouldn't be the last time I experienced a trigger during therapy. It's one of the reasons many people avoid therapy. The great thing about CET is that there is no need to relive the past trauma.

Group therapy for victims of domestic violence

If you have ever experienced some form of trauma, you might have been encouraged to attend group therapy. I was sceptical: I didn't think of myself as a 'victim', nor was my experience 'domestic violence' in the way people normally understand the term, but I went anyway.

We met weekly in a community centre. We sat in a circle and each woman would share her story of being beaten, hit, pushed or punched. They'd been hospitalised, lost teeth and had bones broken. Each woman focused on what had happened. Who had done what to whom. After several weeks, I noticed a pattern. There might have been small variations each week, but the focus was always on what had happened and whose fault it was. The common cry was, 'It's not your fault.' (It was *his*, we repeatedly told each other.)

We repeated the same pattern week after week. We shared, we cried, we sympathised. We even recommended physical solutions (shelters, financial support), but there was no real resolution to the emotional damage. Later, I would learn that sharing, crying, sympathising and offering physical solutions are coping strategies, which are like pills that treat our symptoms without addressing the underlying condition. I observed that while sharing stories and naming our victimisers could feel cathartic and supportive in the moment, it didn't seem to be effecting any long-lasting change. Why wasn't anyone feeling better?

Perhaps because the goal of group therapy isn't necessarily to heal individuals from pain. Instead, according to a standard handbook on the practice,[6] group therapy creates a safe space where individuals can explore their

---

6. ID Yalom and M Leszcz, *Theory and Practice of Group Psychotherapy*, 5th edition (Basic Books, 2005)

situation and allows catharsis through the sharing and expressing of their feelings and experience. Although these benefits sound good, they weren't enough for me. It's true that in my group therapy, no one was judged for being or doing something 'wrong', but there was judgement in the room. We devoted a lot of energy to judging our violent abusers (even the term 'abuser' is a judgement). Let me be clear: what happened to these women – what happened to me – was wrong. I am not saying that we should excuse violence or let perpetrators off the hook for their behaviours. I just wasn't convinced that the group therapy strategies were going to make the pain stop. I was disconcerted by the labels of 'victim' or 'survivor'. I wanted a better, healthier and happier life and neither label really promised that. Offering coping strategies was like patching up a leaky hole. I wanted to feel whole, not patched.

Simply expressing our emotions does not release them. This is why many people stay in talking therapies for years. 'Talking it out', even with a professional, can certainly provide relief, but if the negative emotion from the past is not released, the relief is temporary. Crying, for example, can release endorphins and give temporary relief, but expressing negative emotions actually reinforces them in your neurology. To release them from our lives safely, we need a proven technique that works on the level of our neurology so that new, positive and empowering thought processes can be installed. This is what CET does.

Psychodrama

It was my mum who suggested I try psychodrama. Psychodrama is a group therapy involving active role-play. One member plays the protagonist, inviting other members to play key roles from painful or confusing situations from the past. The drama is frequently paused, discussed and replayed in ways that change the outcomes and behaviours. With the support of the group, active role-playing gives new perspectives on the past, as well as helping the members to access new resources and practise new behaviours. I found a week-long group retreat at a healing centre in Spain and booked it. I was terrified. It brought up almost all of my fears: travelling, travelling alone, not speaking the language and, worst of all, meeting unfamiliar people and sharing a room with one of them. I went anyway.

Just getting myself there was traumatic in itself. During the first session, I had no idea how it worked. I made a mistake in the first group share. I don't recall what I did wrong, but I was interrupted and corrected. I couldn't speak for the rest of the morning. The group leaders were professional and competent, but it was the overwhelming love, support and acceptance of the other members that made the process useful. Psychodrama gave me strategies that helped me cope and offered me some measure of healing and resolution. I went on several more week-long workshops. Although I had new resources and perspectives, I still had to consciously work on situations that challenged me to avoid drowning in my painful emotions. I loved the group connection, but I sensed that better results were possible.

By reliving past events with access to these resources, psychodrama can release the emotions and heal past events. What it can't do is heal every single similar event; it works on one event at a time. This means that it can be slow, and it can also be uncomfortable to re-experience events if they were extremely painful.

Shamanic healing

Shamanic healing entered my world through a series of serendipitous events. I met a woman at a psychodrama workshop who recommended a healing retreat. I booked a few days at the retreat. It was nuts. Crystals and flower essences...Remember, this was the early 90s, so these ideas were a long way from the mainstream. Plus, I was an engineer – we like things we can touch, or better still, kick and hit!

Over an evening meal, I met a Native American woman who started telling me about her healing and spiritual beliefs. She did it in such respectful, non-dogmatic way, filled with evidence, anecdotes and explanations, that I was entranced. She advised me to 'experiment with it', with the caveat: 'Don't believe me because I say it's so. My medicine is my medicine. You must find your medicine.' Armed with some suggested books and a list of recommended training courses, I started my journey around the shamanic medicine wheel. I learned and experienced dream work, energy work, symbolism, soul retrieval, power animals, medicine tools and the use of altered states of consciousness. Something powerful was happening. I experienced some massive shifts – bigger than with any other form of healing so far.

In particular, the idea of healing by removing 'negative energy' from our energy system was potent and compelling. It certainly worked, and the engineer in me set about dismantling the processes to find out how and why. Using the processes of shamanism itself, I travelled to other dimensions and realities to meet with the spirit of shamanism itself. There, I invited it to reveal its secrets, which it eventually did. (I applied these powerful techniques to CET, but more of that to follow.)

Meditation

Not technically a healing modality, according to a significant number of properly controlled studies, meditation has been proven to improve mental health. The results also show that meditation increases health, vitality, energy levels and emotional resilience.[7] 'Worth a try,' I thought.

---

7.   JC Smith, 'Meditation as psychotherapy: A review of the literature', Psychological Bulletin, 82/4 (1975), 558–564, https://doi.org/10.1037/h0076888

Meditation allows us to train our minds to gain control over our thoughts. The idea isn't to silence the mind. The idea is that by giving the mind something to rest on, our thoughts will come to rest on their own. (Or they won't, and that's fine, too.) Meditation allows us to just be aware of our thoughts and notice them without judgement.

The first time I meditated, and every time since then, I experienced waves of pleasure rolling through my brain. I later learned that meditation can release the same endorphins that are released during orgasm. Within four days of learning to meditate, I noticed a difference:

- I was speaking up for myself.

- I stopped apologising.

- I started to have more confidence and became more assertive.

Then the weird shit started. Things continued to get weirder and weirder. I was speaking to dead people, feeling energy and illness and hearing people's thoughts. I started to see auras. What's more, I started to predict the future, and I developed intuitive medical abilities – I could see if someone had cancer or some other serious illness even before it manifested in their physical body. As an engineer, I didn't understand it, but the evidence and experiences were undeniable. Meditation was enabling me to access greater resources – my own resources that I hadn't been able to tap into. Accessing your personal resources is a powerful and important step to healing trauma with CET.

Getting closer...

I then tried several closely related therapies: neurolinguistic programming (NLP), hypnosis, EFT, EmoTrance, Time Line Therapy™ (TLT), and Higher Self therapy (HST), each of which contributed to my breakthrough discovery of CET.

EFT[8] (also known as 'tapping') and EmoTrance both use the theory of 'releasing' energy by tapping or flowing it through the body.[9] I experienced some emotional release, but I found it too uncomfortable to bring significant events into my conscious awareness and hold them there for the time required to release them. EFT and EmoTrance can only release the emotion from one event, memory or situation at a time – another limitation I struggled with. It worked, but it was slow and painful. My instincts told me that there was surely something out there that could work more efficiently and with less pain.

I stumbled across NLP during a professional development training course. NLP is a collection of techniques

---

8. S Hartmann, *Positive EFT: Stronger, faster, smarter, but most of all happier* (DragonRising, 2013)
9. S Hartmann, *Oceans of Energy: The patterns and techniques of EmoTrance* (DragonRising, 2003)

based on modelling successful therapists and therapies. A neurological approach, NLP works from the premise that our brains can be reprogrammed. (Although, it turns out, it doesn't work quite like that.) I found NLP's focus on the structure or process rather than the content of the problem compelling. There wasn't any need to relive the traumatic events of my past in detail or explore what happened, who did what or who said what. Instead, NLP focuses on the meaning applied during a painful event and on the patterns of thought and behaviours that were installed as a result. NLP teaches that we can then use certain processes and techniques to change those thoughts. The beauty is that once installed, these new thoughts run automatically without effort. It is quick and effective.

NLP successfully allowed me to access more resources and cope with situations that had previously caused me great anxiety. I kept studying and practising until I became a certified trainer of NLP, and I have drawn on many NLP techniques in the healing models I have since developed. NLP and hypnosis were a perfect companion to shamanic healing. They both approached mental health from converging, and sometimes overlapping, perspectives.

Time Line Therapy™ is a branch of NLP.[10] TLT is a specific set of techniques and should not be confused

---

10. T James and W Woodsmall, *Time Line Therapy And The Basis Of Personality* (Crown House Publishing, 2017)

with Time Line or 'walking the timeline' often taught in NLP trainings and used for other reasons. TLT is a powerful technique for releasing painful emotions from the past, but the process can be harder and longer for some than for others. It's easy to overthink the process by *trying* to make it work rather than *allowing* it to work. It can reliably change how we feel, but feeling better doesn't always translate into behavioural change.

HST is a technique originating from Huna, a form of shamanic healing developed by the mid-twentieth century American writer, Max Freedom Long.[11] HST was even more effective than TLT. It was quicker and without some of the overthinking issues of TLT, but lacked any specific explanation of how emotions are 'released', making its core concepts difficult to define or describe. Some clients simply can't make the leap of faith needed for HST to work properly.

In a sense, TLT and HST exemplify the fundamental problem I kept encountering on my healing quest – neurological and energetic approaches on one hand, psycho and spiritual approaches on the other. Where was the model that could address both?

---

11. M Freedom Long, *The Secret Science Behind Miracles* (Wildside Press, 2009)

SIX

Eureka! Spiritual And Scientific Fusion

At first glance, a PhD in engineering and a post as a senior lecturer in engineering might not seem the background for a spiritual development teacher; but it was, in many ways, perfect.

Firstly, let's bust the myth that scientists and engineers aren't 'spiritual'. They might not publicly admit to spirituality, but privately, they would admit to believing some unusual things. I'd had many conversations with academics who described strange events and experiences bordering on the paranormal. Engineers, in particular, would talk about certain machines having a personality and some operators 'getting on with them' better than others. Stories of ghosts, telekinesis, telepathy and sightings of strange beings when alone late at night in the lab were not uncommon. It's in the nature of science to be open, but these were only shared in private.

I can pinpoint the day my life split when I was in conversation with a fellow researcher and my hands started to burn. I became aware that he was in pain. When I questioned him, he described a killer back pain and I asked if it was OK if I tried something. 'Sure,' he said. I held my hands over his back and found that some areas felt hotter than others. I held my hands over the hottest area for a few moments, allowing my intuition to guide me. After a few minutes he said he felt much better and asked what I had done. I had to reply, 'I have no idea.' We went back to discussing Bessel functions and their application to modelling traffic flow.

I began to offer readings to people. The next evolution from healing, readings, coaching and therapy was teaching. Many people said to me they wished they were psychic, but they didn't believe they had the gift. By now, I knew that having a gift had nothing to do with it. It was all about training, practice, learning the right skills and removing blocks such as limiting beliefs and negative emotions. I developed an entire model for teaching anyone to connect spiritually: The Mechanics of the Soul.

Total trauma recovery

If anything, I loved training even more than the one-to-one work I had been doing with clients. Of course, I still loved the buzz of hearing a client share how their life had changed, but now I felt I was making an even bigger difference. Becoming a certified trainer in NLP, TLT and hypnosis complemented the spiritual development courses I had been delivering for some time now.

On one occasion, I finished an exercise to release anger using TLT in the usual way by asking, 'How did that exercise go? What questions do you have?' A student replied, 'I was working with Claire and after we released anger, she asked what she should fill the space left by the anger with?' This wasn't the first time this question had arisen. I often found clients getting stuck on the notion that now that something had been removed, if they didn't fill the space with something else, the negative emotion and energy would simply come back.

I used various ways to explain why we don't have empty spaces that need filling, but the question still persisted. Was it just a common myth, or was there something else? Was I missing something? After more research and more experimenting, I discovered something utterly profound: a new process and a way of understanding emotions, love and even the human condition. My trauma, painful emotions and self-esteem issues all dissolved overnight. I didn't have to relive traumatic memories, which also made the therapy gentle and completely safe. At no time did I have to 'face my fears'. I simply let the emotion go and it was, indeed, gone.

The result was like flicking a switch. I was able to be around men and feel OK about it. I was able to speak up for myself and ask for what I wanted or needed. Most importantly, the flashbacks stopped instantly and never came back. As someone who had been haunted daily by her past, was barely able to function normally, and who found even the most ordinary situations traumatic and terrifying, this discovery was nothing short of a miracle.

Furthermore, I *knew and felt* that I was a good person. I didn't deserve what happened to me in the past. I was even able to forgive my abuser. What had I discovered that brought me to a place of such profound and lasting healing?

Love will CET you free

As I went back to first principles and started digging deeper, I realised the fundamental limitation that constrains modern healing modalities. This was when I finally understood that everything I'd tried was *either* psychologically focused (at the expense of the spiritual) *or* spiritually focused (at the expense of our psychology).

Take a look at the Venn diagram below. In the left circle of the Venn diagram, we have therapies that approach the problem of painful emotions from the past, or trauma, from a psychological perspective: NLP, Time Line Therapy™, hypnosis, psychotherapy, psychology and counselling. On the right (or spiritual side), we have therapies such as EFT, ThetaHealing®, Quantum healing, shamanic healing and Reiki.

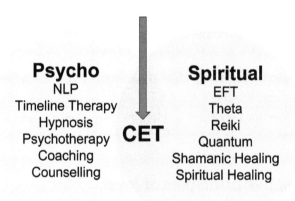

Psycho
NLP
Timeline Therapy
Hypnosis
Psychotherapy **CET**
Coaching
Counselling

Spiritual
EFT
Theta
Reiki
Quantum
Shamanic Healing
Spiritual Healing

I needed to develop an entirely new healing process that lived at the intersection of psychological and spiritual healing: a psycho-spiritual process.

The profound insight I gained led to an even more powerful adaptation of the spiritual healing technology I had been using. I applied several fundamental spiritual *and* psychological principles. This is when I arrived at the Five Principles of Love.

The five principles showed me how to create a working, reliable model for trauma recovery that achieves in a matter of hours what other therapies might take years, if ever, to achieve. I had discovered CET, the one therapy that could efficiently target the Source of emotional trauma while also working on *all subsequent pain* and traumatic events, allowing total trauma recovery. With this unique combination of central concepts, I achieved more profound results than with any individual technique or approach on its own.

When I was finally able to name the five principles that became the basis for CET, I realised why nothing else before had worked so cleanly, completely and swiftly.

The five principles of love

I quickly understood that the breakthrough wasn't just the existence of the principles. On its own, each principle is interesting, but it's the *combination* of these principles that makes CET unique as a psycho-spiritual healing technique. CET not only heals what's broken; with the fifth principle, it allows us to expand, grow and evolve. It's this final and powerful attribute of CET that fulfils the fifth principle of love, making it more a process for transformation than just a therapy.

Conscious Emotional Transformation:

- Finds the resistance to energy
- Removes *all* resistance
- Releases entire histories of trauma
- Rebalances the backlog of energy
- Creates *new neural pathways* that allow more energy to flow
- Returns us to Source

CET enables, facilitates and creates growth and expansion. It is not only remedial but also generative. These principles explain every painful, uncomfortable observation of the human experience, showing us why bad things happen to good people, why good people do bad things and how forgiveness is possible. In the next section, I'll break down each concept and explain why and how it forms a necessary part of CET, but these concepts go way beyond CET: when we get to the end of this explanation, you'll have a new way of thinking about your – humanity's – entire existence.

Principle 1: There is only love

I have said it many times throughout this book, and I will say it again: there is only one emotional energy, or emotion, and it is love. You might not use the word 'love' – if you have a word you prefer, simply replace 'love' with any term you feel more comfortable with. The idea that there is only love isn't new, nor is it mine. Many spiritual texts teach this, but I have a slightly different approach that starts to bring everything together.

Let's start with the idea that there is *only one* emotion, and that it's love. What we feel as love, or joy or something positive is what we feel when love flows through us. Yet, love is more than simply a feeling. Love can be described as E-motion. Energy in motion. It's an emotional energy, or simply, a form of energy. Any spiritual philosophies and modes of healing include the concept of a 'universal lifeforce' energy. You might have heard of terms like:

- Prana
- Chi
- Information
- Akasha
- Energy
- LAO (Iaō)
- Universal energy
- Source energy
- God

Love makes things happen. It causes us to take action. Love is what we feel or experience when energy moves through our being.

Principle 2: Everything is energy

The entire universe, and everything in it, is made of energy. Everything is love (or Source, unity, God…) Energy is neither negative nor positive. It is simply energy. Through energy, we are all connected. This concept is fairly universally accepted. The concept of wave-particle duality in quantum physics,[12] for example, states that matter is a probability function which can either appear as a wave made up of energy, or physical matter. If we attempt to measure a particle as a wave, it behaves as an energy wave with no mass. If we attempt to measure a particle's mass, we find it has mass. If particles collide, they bounce off one another. If waves collide, they pass through each other. To further confound us, when we attempt to locate the particle, it shows up exactly where we measure it. Like a naughty child dancing around a room when we're not looking, matter is a particle and a wave, and everywhere all at once, until we turn around and look (measure it), and then it decides to behave properly, sitting down where we asked it to and have mass or be a wave as we've told it to.

Authors Amit Goswami, Fritjof Capra, Michael Talbot, and Deepak Chopra have all written excellent

---

12. Amit Goswami, *Physics of the Soul* (Hampton Roads Publishing, 2013); Fritjof Capra, *The Tao of Physics* (HarperCollins Publishers, 1992); Deepak Chopra, *Quantum Healing,* revised edition (Bantam Dell, 2015); Michael Talbot, *The Holographic Universe*, revised edition (HarperCollins Publishers, 1996)

books on the topic of the energetic universe (see note 12). The original research includes that of Max Planck, Schrödinger, de Broglie and Heisenberg.

Around the time when I first learned that the universe is infinite Source energy, the same teacher explained the concepts of negative energy and the importance of 'psychic protection'. She spoke about identifying and removing evil spirits and negative energy. Many spiritual circles tout the importance of cleaning our auras, rooms and places, focusing on the idea of clearing ourselves from this negativity. It often feels like a war is being waged on 'negative energy'. I was confused by what I was hearing from friends and teachers. I would ask, 'What makes energy negative? How is it different from positive energy? How can we be sure energy is negative or positive?' My analytical mind noticed a contradiction: if evil is that which is *not* God or Source, but everything is God or Source, then how can evil exist? I started to question the nature of evil. What was it? How did we define it? What made some energy 'positive' and some 'negative'? What were the criteria for this definition?

Despite my questioning, I never got a satisfactory answer. It seemed to me then, and it seems to me now, too simplistic to simply label these behaviours, situations and acts as 'evil'. This easy categorisation directly contradicts the principle of an infinite, Source-filled universe. It then requires all kinds of mental gymnastics to explain how this all-loving Source could not only allow evil to exist, but also *be* evil. Either everything *is* Source, or it's not. How can we reconcile this? Of course, our experience demonstrates that there are situations filled with pain, both physical and emotional. We can observe anger, fear, guilt, rage, wrath, greed and self-ishness everywhere. Leaders bully and manipulate. People gleefully trample on others to get ahead. This is undeniable.

How does any of this make sense or have any purpose? I thought about energy from an engineer's perspective – a scientist's perspective. As a lecturer in thermo-dynamics, I explored the idea of energy as a thought experiment. Thermal energy, kinetic energy, potential energy...Certainly, we can find energy in different forms, and some forms are more useful than others, but it's still always energy in one form or another. In and of itself, energy has no bias, no ideology, no moral compass – it isn't positive or negative.

OK, but I still wasn't satisfied. One day, my washing machine broke. I called for a repair operative who dis-covered a single £1 coin had escaped from a pocket and lodged in a duct, blocking it. Money was to blame. That same week, due to some poor accounting, I inadvert-ently allowed my bank account to go overdrawn and I was charged a small fee. The amount I'd overdrawn was...You guessed it: £1. The money itself wasn't good or evil. It was simply *in the wrong place*. Had the £1 been in my account and not the washing machine, I could have saved myself a lot of distress.

This got me thinking. Maybe that's how emotions work? What if love is the only emotion? What if all those things my teachers warned me against – all the energies and forces I needed to protect myself from or cleanse away – are just love energy in the wrong place? What if negative emotions and bad behaviour are just love energy in the wrong place?

Principle 3: The infinite, energetic self

Just as the universe is an infinite Source of interconnected energy, every individual is an infinite being, with an infinite number of channels through which emotional energy can flow. In almost every spiritual, energy, esoteric and even religious philosophy, you'll find some version of the idea that you are an infinite soul (also known as your ineffable self, Higher Self, soul or divine essence).

Much of the pain and unhappiness we experience in life is caused when we forget or lose contact with the knowledge that we are divine. Although we might understand and accept our divine inner essence as an abstract idea, many of us rarely go further than that, leaving us stuck in the small version of ourselves. We feel limited because of our how our mind works. This is sometimes referred to as 'spiritual pain'.

The Mechanics of the Soul

We can think of our consciousness (soul, being, essence) as not one thing, but existing in three parts: the

conscious mind, the *unconscious mind* and the *Higher Self.*
Although I use the word 'mind', I am not referring to
the brain in an anatomical or physiological way (even
though our brain plays a central part in storing information and emotions). When I use 'mind', I mean the
levels of awareness that make up our psyche, our soul.
It's important to note that these are not three separate
entities, but rather three distinct aspects of your whole
being and awareness. Each of the three minds depend
on the others.

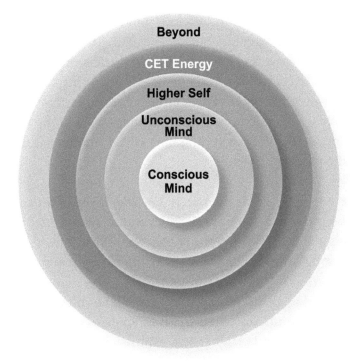

The *conscious mind* is the part of us that experiences
reality; it's also the part of us that chooses and decides

what's real. Our conscious mind is everything we pay attention to in our present moment of awareness. It allows us to focus; it is the home of rational thought, judgements, decisions and assessments. It is our free will. The conscious mind isn't fixed; our present moment of awareness can change at any moment and can move between our past (memories), our immediate present moment and our future (hopes, dreams, fears, etc).

The opposite of your conscious mind is your *unconscious mind*, which contains all the stuff that you're not conscious of. Our unconscious mind contains our personal programming, beliefs and patterns, emotional blueprints, strategies and skills. While these things are usually completely outside of our conscious awareness, we live their effects in our choices, beliefs and behaviours. Memories and emotions reside in the unconscious mind, including unresolved emotions from the past and trauma.

Your *Higher Self* is the part of you that is pure Source/Love/Divine. Inspiration and intuition flow from the Higher Self. *You are* your Higher Self, expressing itself through the lens of *your* personality in physical form.

A human is the integration of all three minds functioning optimally together. Thus, you are infinite. You are your Infinite Higher Self, expressing itself through your unconscious mind, consciously aware of yourself via your conscious mind. This is a *vital* concept that deserves its own book, but you can find out more here: www.cetfreedom.com

Many of us can accept a concept of our innate divinity abstractly, but we don't feel it in our daily lives. Why? We feel disconnected from the more infinite versions of ourselves when our three minds are not integrated – when there's been a breakdown in how they communicate and share information with each other.

When we store our trauma and emotional pain in our unconscious mind, we create the blocks that prevent our ERC from running smoothly, impeding the free flow of love energy (as we saw in Chapters 3 and 4). When our unconscious mind harbours old pain, we are not only less able to feel and experience love, but we also become increasingly disconnected from our unconscious mind and Higher Self. We are left with only our conscious mind as our regular companion. Our conscious mind is finite and limited, so we feel limited. Finite.

Part of the work we do in CET is to re-open the channels of communication between the conscious and unconscious minds, allowing that glorious flow of pure love from your Higher Self to pour into every aspect of your life, reconnecting you to your infinite and divine true self.

Principle 4: Love hurts (when it meets resistance)

The experience we call feeling a negative emotion is caused by the absence of love or the resistance to love. What we feel as a negative emotion is actually the experience of resisting the flow of love energy.

If we are truly infinite beings with an infinite number of possible neural pathways, and if love is truly an energetic force, then every second of every hour of every day, love energy is attempting to flow throughout our energy body, along the pathways of our neurology.

Resistance, block, break...There are many terms we could use to describe how we resist love. It's common to use the word 'block', but it isn't actually possible (yet) to identify a physical break or block in the nervous system. Any term or concept that describes the experience of preventing the flow of love will work. It's a metaphor. Imagine each channel in the nervous system is a river in which love flows. If we were to dam the river, we would end up with a pool of water on the upstream side and a dried-up river bed on the downstream side. A build-up of love that can't get out on one side, and another side desperately in need of love. It's this difference in the levels of energy that we feel and label as some kind of 'negative feeling'. Our anatomy is designed to notice these build-ups/congestions and depletions.

Take the example of our nervous systems. Imagine you're a sailor on a submarine. The engines are quietly (or possibly quite loudly), but constantly, chugging away. Sailors on a submarine will sleep, read, talk through and over the noise of the engine. It's there in the background as a constant rumble or roar. The nervous system learns to adapt and no longer brings it into conscious awareness; but when the engines stop, speed up, or the volume or pitch of the engine noise changes by even a small amount, the whole crew will become alert to find the cause of the change. It's the same with the flow of emotional energy or love through the nervous system. As long as the love energy is flowing, we don't notice it. When its flow is hindered for any reason, we notice it. What we notice is the *change* or the *difference* and we label it.

We do so love to label our emotions. As artists and poets remind us, we humans have a nuanced vocabulary for describing our human experience, including our negative emotions. All the negative emotions that we feel are, ultimately, either a resistance to love, or an attempt to hold on to love. Let's look at the five most common categories of negative emotions:

- Anger is what we feel when love is withheld, when we don't get the love we deserve, or when someone does something unloving.

- Sadness is what we feel when we lose something, or someone, we love.

- Fear is what we feel when think we will, or might, lose love or that we are not loved.

- Hurt is what we feel when love is withheld or when our attempt to give love is rejected.

- Guilt is what we feel when we think we did not love another enough or we did something unloving.

Let's take the emotion we commonly label 'hurt'. When we love someone or experience a loving exchange, we will lovingly do something for another. We might give them a gift, embrace them, recite a sappy poem or invite them to dinner. We want to *give* love to them. We are attempting to create the flow between us. However, when our gifts are refused, our overtures rebuffed or we don't get invited to the party, we experience hurt. The flow of love is hindered.

Ideally, this would happen only in the present moment, and we would lovingly notice that our words or actions are not getting the results we want. We would change our actions, words and behaviours to allow the flow of love to resume. Our emotional feedback (warmer/cooler) mechanism that we've called the ERC would run beautifully and our icky feelings in the present would let us know that this action, this situation we find ourselves in, is the opposite to what we desire. These emotions are not only not a problem, they are also highly useful. They are life's warning lights and alarm signals giving us vital feedback. However, when we find ourselves still feeling bad about something from the past and the feeling interferes with our life's purpose and our capacity to experience joy and love, that's a sign that something else is going on: our ERC is looping and failing to complete satisfactorily. When this happens, we suffer. We experience trauma in our neurology that we feel as pain.

Principle 5: Love seeks love

We are evolving beings, always changing and becoming better. Love seeks to grow and evolve and experience.

Let's recap: Source is infinite energy. Each individual is an expression of Source, and Source expresses itself and experiences itself *through* us. If Source wishes to express more of itself, it makes sense that it would seek to grow and expand through us. Anywhere and any time there is resistance to love, we are throttling Source; we are blocking Source. Beautifully, the opposite is also true: anywhere and any time we expand and grow and enable Source to experience more of itself, we are fulfilling our divine purpose, and we experience this as joy, bliss and love.

SEVEN
How To CET Yourself Free

I looked out at the audience and went into what I called 'stage mode'. It was automatic now, after thousands of hours of delivering live trainings and speaking from the stage. I had my crew and sound engineers and I was mic'd up. I had a hair and make-up artist who made me look and feel gorgeous. This event was no different to any other, really, but it felt different.

It felt different because this one was in Southampton – a city I had lived in during my previous life as an engineer and academic. I seemed to have come full circle. Here I was, speaking to just under 300 delegates who were interested in learning about raising their consciousness and emotional resilience. They wanted to hear my story. They were interested in learning about CET and the other spiritual and personal empowerment techniques I taught.

When I'd lived in Southampton, I'd probably looked as if I lived a normal, happy life, but on the inside, I had been struggling – silently and invisibly – with painful emotions and limiting decisions from my past. It seemed significant to be back in a place where I had been in so much pain and was now feeling so much joy – not only at being here and because of the work I was doing, but also in my personal life. I have a fabulous husband, and we have a joyful relationship. I have a beautiful daughter who is happy, healthy and also in a loving relationship with her partner. I have great friends. I do fun things. I live a joyful life, and now I had the opportunity to share with these people how they could also live a life of joy.

How and why CET works

To recap, CET is a unique healing modality because it:

- Finds the origin of trauma in blocks throughout our ERC
- Removes and repairs *all* resistance throughout the ERC
- Quickly removes *all* emotional pain from the past at once
- Rebalances our energetic flow
- Creates new neural pathways, allowing *more* energy to flow
- Returns us to Source

Now I will explain *how* the CET process actually works and what you can expect from a CET intervention. This is not a 'how-to' or DIY guide. My goal is to give you a general sense of how we perform CET, but the actual process can only be performed by trained CET practitioners.

CET finds resistance

One of the things that makes CET different is our focus on the cause rather than the symptoms. During the first part of a CET intervention, you will be guided by your practitioner to bring your emotional triggers into awareness and to find your limiting belief. You'll be clearing the block without needing to analyse how you feel about the block. You'll be working with the block itself and not the triggers caused by the block.

We accomplish this by gently (and completely without judgement) asking you some deep and penetrating questions to pinpoint where and when the resistance in the neurology is located. The origins of blocks are in what we call the 'first event'. This is the moment when a block was installed, your ERC was prevented from completing, and it created the painful emotion(s) you are currently experiencing. To help find your triggers and identify your first event, you will be given some exercises. This is the least comfortable part of the process, but we don't linger there.

Your CET practitioner will give you a list of the major emotions – anger, sadness, fear, hurt, guilt – and ask you to make a list of everything that currently triggers those emotions. You don't need to analyse or understand them. You simply list them by completing the sentences below:

- I'm angry about…

- Things that make me sad are…

- I'm afraid of…

- I've been hurt by…

- I'm guilty of…

It is extremely powerful to find the root cause of the resistance, ie, the limiting belief which applied some inappropriate meaning to an event in the past (remember Phase 2 of the ERC). For most people, the first event is actually quite minor – usually a phrase or statement that is fundamentally limiting – but enough to install a block. Repeated over time with numerous painful events, each of which might actually be much more significant, what may have begun as a minor incident takes on the weight of deeper trauma.

Think of it this way: when one tiny twig gets stuck in the flow of a river, it creates a small, but significant, block. Over time, more leaves, twigs, branches and debris are trapped behind that tiny twig until a whole dam has built up around it. The tiny twig is now insignificant compared with the much larger dam. We might not even remember when and how that one tiny twig got stuck, but it's like a lynch pin holding the entire dam(n!) structure in place: tug it loose and the whole thing will fall apart, releasing and rebalancing the flow of water.

The distinction between a first event and the experiences that follow is significant and is one way in which CET is different from other therapies. In other kinds of therapies, healing often focuses on the later, larger events or the repetition of certain painful emotions and experiences, when the root of the problem is elsewhere all along – in a first event that may not even be in your conscious awareness. In CET, you don't need to remember what happened. You don't need to feel and re-experience all that pain. In fact, there's increasing research which suggests that reliving traumatic memories can often make things worse.[13] Each time you relive or recount a traumatic event, you reinforce the damage in your neural pathways. In contrast, our work aims to uncover the first, probably minor or mild, event where all the trouble began.

Imagine that you have a stone in your shoe and it's painful. To stop the pain, you wouldn't analyse your shoe, the kind of stone or the ground you were walking

---

13. S Nolen-Hoeksema, BE Wisco and S Lyubomirsky, 'Rethinking rumination', *Perspectives in Psychological Science*, 3 (2008), 400–424, https://doi.org/10.1111/j.1745-6924.2008.00088.x

on at the time. You wouldn't study weather patterns, or what you were thinking about at the time or what you ate the day before. You'd simply stop walking, take off your shoe and remove the stone. That's how CET works. It just removes the stone, or resistance, that's causing the pain. You don't need to know anything about *why* or *how* it got there. This is why CET is so effective: we only need to find and remove that tiny twig and the dam will break all by itself.

CET removes *all* resistance

Resistance is anything that stops the flow of love energy. You can use a variety of metaphors to help you conceptualise resistance – a block, a clog, a break, a disconnection – it doesn't actually matter. What matters is that the CET practitioner uses this energetic process to remove, restore, reconnect and repair. All you have to do is pay attention to the emotion and resistance, and you'll notice it starts to go.

What do I mean by 'pay attention to the emotion'? Didn't I just promise you that you wouldn't have to relive any painful moments or memories with CET? Let me explain.

Remember that CET can only remove emotions that you are conscious of. A CET practitioner knows how to safely and gently bring an emotion from your unconscious mind into your conscious mind to remove it.

This might sound uncomfortable, but for the vast majority of clients, it's far less painful than they imagined. Being consciously aware of an emotion is different from reliving or re-experiencing it. You are simply becoming aware of the emotional pain that you are likely to be experiencing all the time. Your conscious mind receives the information from the unconscious mind and responds with something like, 'Oh, there's some anger/hurt/fear/guilt here.' At the precise moment that you bring the emotional pain into awareness, your CET practitioner guides your unconscious mind to access the CET energy and instantly dissolves resistance and restores energy and emotional imbalances. *You will not replay any traumatic events*. Your conscious mind will only hold the awareness for about ninety seconds. That's nothing compared to the vast amounts of time, energy and attention most people spend vainly trying to avoid it.

CET clears your entire past

As we learned earlier, for most of us, the first event that created the original problem in our ERC was minor and relatively insignificant. The subsequent events may be far more painful, significant or even traumatic than the first event. While most therapies help us work through those more obvious and painful events, they don't address the true origin of past pain. Furthermore, they usually only work on one emotionally charged event at a time. Only CET can quickly and efficiently get to the Source, which may be so minor that it's currently outside of your conscious awareness.

'But how can an event so small that I don't remember it or am not aware of it cause so much pain, especially when I've experienced other, much more traumatic stuff?' you may be asking. It's a great question.

Reprogrammed

It only takes a small amount of resistance in our ERC to create a bigger block, more resistance, and, subsequently, more pain. Each time that the ERC can't run because of resistance, further blocks and resistance build up. Because CET clears the block at the level of the first event and releases all the built-up resistance, any subsequent and significant events are cleared in the same process. There's no need to directly address each significant traumatic event in turn, which is how most healing modalities operate. CET clears *all* the emotional pain from *all* subsequent trauma. A story from my early days as an engineer illustrates my point:

In the beginning of my engineering career, I had a summer job in a bottling factory. Corks were placed into bottles by a machine on the production line, but the machine wasn't getting it quite right: about 5 mm of cork stood proud of the bottle neck. Someone decided that the best solution was to manually tap down the corks into the bottles using a rubber hammer. This was my job. To say this was boring is an understatement. Tap. Tap. Tap. I tapped every cork into every bottle.

During a tea break, I noticed the grey cabinet which housed the Programmable Logic Controller (PLC). The PLC is a simple computer that controls machines in a production line. Without being asked, I opened up the PLC cabinet, got into the controller and started scrolling through the lines of code that controlled the corking machine. I was pretty confident that I could figure out a way to get the corks inserted properly and eliminate the need to pound them with a rubber hammer.

I found a line that determined the 'stroke length' (is that yet another engineering double entendre, like 'grease nipples' and 'busty couplings'?) and adjusted it. My first go was unsuccessful. The machine pounded the cork so far down that it broke the bottle. (Several, in fact, before I could shut it off.) I went back and adjusted the code again. After more trial and error, I made the right adjustment to the programming. The corks now landed perfectly in their bottles and no longer needed hammering. (Yes, I ended up being sacked, because I had made myself redundant.)

My point is that this is how CET works. CET reprogrammes the machine so that the line runs smoothly. You don't need someone to hit the corks with a rubber hammer. You don't need coping strategies or need to avoid triggers. You don't need to even think about the past or your problem again. Your unconscious mind and neurology have been permanently and perfectly reprogrammed.

UNHAND THAT SNACK

Lorna wanted to lose weight and quit smoking, but she always had to have something in her mouth. If she wasn't smoking, she was snacking. She ate or smoked while she was driving, watching TV, etc. Her desk at work had a dedicated snack drawer that was always kept full. She worked really hard to limit her calorie intake and keep to only one packet of cigarettes a day, but it was a never-ending effort.

'I'll wait just ten minutes, then eat something or smoke,' she would tell herself, but it was an agonising effort of willpower for her. Stress only made things worse.

Once we'd done the preliminary work to find the triggers and root cause limiting belief, I took her through the CET release. It went really well. On cue, she had an epiphany about a traumatic event when she was six and comfort-ate for the first time: after something particularly upsetting happened, she had gone upstairs to her room and scoffed every single one of her Christmas chocolates in one secret sitting. She'd eaten until she was sick. This was the beginning of her pattern.

A month later, we had a follow-up call. 'I've had to stop buying snacks,' she said excitedly. 'Initially, I thought it hadn't worked and I kept buying snacks, but then I realised my pantry cupboard was full. My desk drawer was full. I've simply stopped snacking altogether. It's not only that I don't snack. I could always stop snacking, but it was so much effort. I haven't even had to try. I'm not constantly at war with myself – I just don't want to snack. It's like you've turned off the snack switch in my head! Now, I just eat normally.'

Several months later, I got an email. 'I've stopped smoking. I was standing by the back door, about to go out and have a cigarette. I looked at the packet and thought, "That's disgusting." I haven't smoked for over three months now.'

This is how CET changes problem programming. You experience the change, without the effort and will-power.

People problems

When you have a problem with the people in your life, it can be caused by your internal belief systems. If you seem unable to resolve it directly with the people in question, it could be that the place to look is within. Finding that limiting belief (or the break in your ERC that is causing repeated problems with others) and clearing it with CET will change your life, your circumstances and even others in your life. You can be sure that your problem is fully resolved within when one of three things happens:

1. The person disappears from your life.

2. The person is still in your life, but no longer displays the triggering behaviour.

3. The person is still in your life, still displaying the inappropriate behaviour, but it no longer triggers you.

Let's look at each of these in turn:

The stalker

There he was. Again. I saw the name blinking on my screen. I was commenting on a post on a new group online. He seemed to be everywhere I went. The comments weren't overtly offensive, just subtly undermining. He questioned everything. He gave unsolicited advice about what I said, my picture, what I wore in my picture, what was on my website and what I was teaching.

I'd been running my spiritual development business for a few years and making enough to hit the VAT threshold. Our courses filled up pretty well. I was getting increasingly written up in the media. Then this guy shows up. He's in every group I'm in. He's in my inbox. He even tries to call me on Skype: just 'wants a chat', whatever that means, and it's creepy. He's not exactly rude or offensive. It would have been easier if he had been. He's just ever so slightly on the wrong side of socially accepted norms – which means I look bad if I call him out. He's just being helpful; he's trying to be nice. Why am I being such a bitch? I tried being polite, both publicly and privately on Messenger. I tried reasoning with him by asking him, as politely as possible, to not comment on every one of my posts. I tried to find out what his motives were. What did he want from me? Did he want to work with me? Was he trying to sell me something? Nothing seemed to work. I knew I could block him, but I also knew that something else was going on.

I explored my belief systems. Based on the assumption that we must be creating or attracting something because of some belief we hold, I have a magic question I ask myself and coaching clients any time we are experiencing something we don't like in our world. I asked myself, 'What must I believe about myself, or the world, that would create this situation?' The answer came back. 'He's always watching you.' I flashed back to the grotty flat, hearing Gary's voice telling me, 'I will always be watching you.' Gary was long out of my life, and I knew he wasn't actually watching me, so what if this was a metaphor for something else? I'd made Gary's words mean that I was, and always would be, watched.

I ran the test. If I believed it to be true that I would always be watched, would an example of that be the behaviour I was experiencing from this creepy online guy? Yes, this experience was exactly what I would create. I released this belief with CET – and he vanished. Simply disappeared. No more posts, no more comments, no more messages (this is now called 'ghosting'). I have never been stalked, watched or had any similar experience since. This is an example of how 'they disappear from your life.'

The convert

'It's just so bloody hard all the time,' Karen said, exasperated. She was describing how her husband gave her 'zero support' in the home. 'He does no housework. Whenever I want to go on a course or travel for work, he just makes it hard. He never seems to be able to take on any childcare. The one time he dropped our daughter off at nursery, he sent her in her pyjamas and without any lunch. I had to leave work, cancel all my meetings and go back and sort it.'

It's not an unusual story. We could accept this as a cultural norm and moan about it but do nothing. Karen had tried having conversations with her husband, but they always ended in arguments. She could simply not get him to accept that her work had any value or merit. His work came first. He earned (only slightly) more than her, but much of her income was swallowed by childcare, so it made little difference to the family income and, according to her husband, was worthless.

'Let's explore this from a beliefs perspective, shall we?' I suggested. 'We'll assume that if we create a situation or experience in our lives, it could be due to a limiting belief (or set of beliefs) which, if we find and delete, will change our external experiences.' Twenty-five minutes later, Karen was slightly tearful at the realisation that she was harbouring these beliefs: I don't matter. I'm worthless. Nothing I do has any value.

We ran the test: If you believed this to be true, and others could somehow pick up on this belief telepathically, would it cause them to treat you the way your husband does? 'Yes, it would,' came the answer. We deleted this belief with CET and transformed it. We also installed a set of new empowering beliefs: I am loved, lovable and loving. I am valuable. What I have to offer has meaning and worth.

Later that night I got an excited, slightly confused, but happy call from Karen. 'You're not going to believe this,' she said. 'Try me.' (I'd heard this before.) 'I went home, and rather than the usual chaos in the house, our daughter had been fed, bathed and was in her jammies ready for bed. The floor had been vacuumed, the dishwasher emptied *and* restacked. He'd gone shopping and cooked a meal, and I mean a nice, healthy, home-cooked meal. I can hardly believe it. I felt like saying, "Who are you and what have you done with my husband? He's been abducted by aliens and replaced by a doppelganger and I love it."'

This is how the 'no longer displays triggering behaviour' scenario might show up. When we release a limiting belief, it's as if others are reading our minds and responding to our new belief system. (Extraordinary as this might seem, there is some early evidence based on quantum biology that our thoughts might actually be doing this.[14] This field of study is in its infancy, as yet unproven and controversial.)

---

14. J Al-Khalili J and McFadden, *Life On The Edge: The coming of age of quantum biology* (Bantam Press, 2014)

Letting it go

My mum's number flashed on the phone's display and I answered. She usually called on a Sunday morning. That had been our pattern for years. Despite living 12,000 miles apart (her in Melbourne, Australia, and me in Cornwall), we maintained a great relationship. I looked forward to our calls. We talked about books, politics, relationships, business, leadership, management, money, investing, people, recipes and knitting patterns.

Sometimes, though, she would get herself into a 'moaning mode', in which she would repeat the same set of phrases about whatever today's topic was. I usually tried to be patient and listen, but I'm human and some days I had fewer resources than others. Since she had been diagnosed with terminal cancer (a cancer that took a long slow and painful three years to finally take her life), her moaning sessions had become more frequent. She didn't want to die, she was in so much pain, she didn't like her oncologist, she didn't like to be a burden to my brother, she didn't want to die. And repeat...

Who could deny a dying woman the time and space to share the burden of her suffering? I would listen, sometimes offering alternative perspectives or suggestions, but knowing she was not open to change. I won't deny that sometimes I found it hard. It's not easy to hear someone you love suffer. I would need hours to decompress after one of her sessions. I always allowed her the time, but it wore me down. I wanted her pain and suffering to stop, so, I did an inner healing. I found some unhelpful beliefs about myself, my energy levels and my own mindset. I transformed them with CET.

Did my mum suddenly morph into a happy-clappy version of herself? No. She still moaned. It could still go on for hours. The difference was how I felt about it. It became an honour and a blessing. I felt lucky that she felt safe and comfortable enough with me to unburden herself. After our calls, I no longer felt drained. I felt as if I had been of some service. One day, she told me how grateful she was that she could talk to me. She couldn't share her suffering with my brother; he already had so much to deal with. He was there on the ground, delivering and organising daily care for her while managing a young family and full-time work. The time, attention and space that I allowed her to unburden herself was my privilege.

After I transformed my belief, she was (for almost another year) still in my life and she still behaved in the same way, but how I felt about it was completely transformed. In a late-night chat, my brother shared how brave she'd been. 'She must have been in so much pain, but she never complained.' She *was* brave. I was lucky to have had such a mum and I'm still lucky to have such a brother. I'm so grateful that I was able to transform how I felt about her during her last year with us; that I could allow her the space to be who she needed to be at that time and that I could be at peace with it.

CET is simple, fast and efficient. It transforms our experience of our lives and the people in it.

EIGHT

The Power Of CET

D an wept and wept. 'Where are you now, Dan?' I asked.

'I'm back at the time my girlfriend left me. That's the event.'

'Good, now open your eyes and look up.' He returned to the present. He'd gone back to a significant event, but that wasn't the *first* event. We were looking for the first time he had felt sadness. 'How old were you when your girlfriend left you?'

'Twenty-two,' Dan answered.

'And that's the first time you felt sadness?' He nodded. 'Let's just think about this logically for a moment. Up until that time, aged twenty-two, you had never, in your entire life, felt sad? Wouldn't you agree that the chances you felt sadness for the first time aged twenty-two are pretty slim?'

'Yes, of course I felt sad before then, it's just that there was so much sadness when she left.'

'I know,' I said gently, 'but can you ask your unconscious mind what the earliest time was that you felt sadness?'

'When I was a baby.' I intuitively felt that we had found the first event.

'Let's go with that then, shall we?'

'But I can't remember what happened!' Dan exclaimed.

'You don't need to know,' I reassured him. 'Remember, it's not what happened, it's not the events that are important; it's how your mind and nervous system responded at the time. All you need to do is trust your unconscious mind and allow it to guide you.'

'OK,' Dan spoke softly.

'Let's clear the sadness then, shall we?' And we did.

Connect with energy

CET rebalances energy

Once the resistance has been removed, your practitioner will guide you and your unconscious mind gently and safely through carefully managed stages to access an infinite Source of energy. You are flooded with love energy. You literally *re*-Source yourself. Your entire being is awash with pure Source energy, with infinite love. This experience is extremely pleasant. Some have described it as blissful or even orgasmically pleasant.

CET creates new energy

There are two reasons why people seek help through coaching or therapy. Either they experience themselves as broken and are seeking healing, or they are mostly OK, but are seeking further growth. For the first group of people, something in their lives is fundamentally off. They may struggle to get or keep a job or have relationship challenges. They are sick, triggered or stuck. They experience problems and are looking to fix something that's not working. We describe this as 'remedial' change. The other group of people experience their lives as fundamentally good. Most things are more or less working, but they seek more. They want their relationships to be even better, more intimate, more connected. They might want a better job, or to grow their business or improve their team or profits.

They seek to generate even more of the good things in their life. We call this 'generative' change.

CET is great for both. I've told you that CET is not only remedial, but also generative. Even if you come to CET for remedial change, CET also *creates* expansion. It enables, facilitates and creates growth and expansion. What do I actually mean by this? Think about a human's energy system as a large number of neurological connections or pathways along which energy and information can flow. When we have more pathways, we open more possibilities. CET helps you to increase your connections and pathways so that the network is greater than it was before. This stage creates new strategies and pathways, behaviours and patterns that are empowered. With more neurological connections, you can be, do and have more.

CET returns you to Source

We could say that all the resistances and blocks we experience are caused by a misunderstanding: forgetting that we are divine. You can refer to this concept in any way that feels comfortable. Whether or not you believe in Source, spirit or God doesn't matter and is not required for CET to work. Maybe you believe in a higher power, a greater part of yourself, or the unconscious mind – whatever you name it, it's this greater, bigger, more powerful, more aware or just 'other' part of you that CET works with. You only need to be willing to accept the notion that there is a part of you that goes beyond physical experience and your conscious mind.

In Chapter 5, the third principle of love teaches us that we are infinite and divine beings, and we know that across the world, many religious and spiritual teachings assert that we are an expression of God on earth. We are divine. Resistance and blocks are the opposite of infinite love and divinity. When we re-Source with CET, we are able to restore our neurology or mindset to its original, infinite state of divine Source.

Freedom from sin

In my years of working with clients who have experienced a wide array of challenges and past trauma, I've noticed a common theme when it comes to root causes and first events. In almost all cases, the root cause of their emotional pain is a limiting belief that they are bad, evil or somehow 'not good enough'. They believe they are sinners and unworthy of divine love, and have separated themselves from their true, infinite state.

This isn't too surprising. In the Abrahamic religions, sin is described as a transgression of God's laws. In the modern world, we tend to understand sin as a bunch of things we should or should not do. These 'dos and don'ts' are listed in our religious books or texts, and if we do (or don't do) according to our holy books, we have sinned. Even if we don't use the word 'sin', the belief that adhering to a set of rules (made by God, gods, the universe, our culture, our parents, etc) determines our worthiness or happiness permeates our human experience.

Let's take another perspective: The literal translation of sin (or 'khatah') from the original, biblical Hebrew is 'to miss the mark'. Perhaps a truer meaning of the word 'sin' is to forget we are divine, or to adopt the mistaken belief that we are not divine? It often shakes down like this. On the one hand, we consciously believe that we are bad, evil, a sinner or unworthy (whatever your terminology is for not measuring up). On the other, we acknowledge that there's a part of us, outside of our conscious awareness, which is divine (or however you experience this). Conversely, maybe we consciously believe that we are divine, but our unconscious mind harbours a deeply rooted limiting belief in our broken, sinful nature. Either way, isn't this a contradiction?

Yes! And our conscious mind knows this. Opposite and opposing beliefs cannot exist simultaneously in our conscious awareness, so one of these limiting beliefs is always outside of our conscious awareness. In CET, we bring the two ideas into your consciousness simultaneously and they act like matter and antimatter – they cancel each other out, destroying the block, and leaving only *you*, in your pure, clear and perfect form. CET washes away all notion of sin and restores us to our divine natures. We feel reunited with, and into, Source – the experience of blissful unity. CET is simple, powerful and easy – on both the practitioner and the client. (If you are into the more metaphysical stuff and want to really understand some of the complex concepts at work here, I encourage you to experience CET free at www.cetfreedom.com or follow me on social media.)

If all this sounds like magic and almost too good to be true, well, simply try it for yourself.

How to help yourself now

Maybe you need some immediate relief from pain, or maybe you aren't yet convinced that CET is for you. What follows are a series of things you can do that will not only give you some relief from the symptoms of trauma, but they will also actually *help* CET to work. Unlike the coping strategies I outlined in Chapter 1 (which actually make it harder for CET to work because they cause you to numb out or dissociate), these techniques *make the process easier, faster and more comfortable*. These simple techniques work by changing your current emotional state. They will increase your self-awareness, including your communication with your unconscious mind and emotions. They will help you to feel calmer and more emotionally aware and balanced, *but* please note that they are temporary stopgaps that will not permanently release blocks or trauma and are in no way intended to replace seeking help from a certified practitioner.

Meditation

Meditation is a process of entering a relaxed, trance-like state. While there are many myths and misconceptions about meditation, its true purpose is to observe your thoughts, and in some cases, guide them rather than stopping or blocking them. Any technique that causes you to observe and guide your thoughts is meditative: breath counting, chanting a mantra or simply observing your thoughts mindfully.

There is significant and growing evidence for the effectiveness of meditation for our mental and physical health.[15] Meditation improves the rapport between your unconscious and conscious minds, giving you greater access to internal resources and awareness. When you practice meditation regularly, you improve your ability to control your thoughts and your subsequent emotional response. This can increase your resourcefulness and help to prevent you from being triggered in the moment.

How to meditate

Sit quietly, close your eyes and bring your awareness to either your breath or a mantra. Any time you find your mind wandering off into thoughts (mundane or traumatic), simply bring your awareness back to your

---

15. DS Khalsa and C Stauth, *Meditation As Medicine: Activate the power of your natural healing* (Atria Books, 2001)

mantra or your breath. Any mantra or sound will do – experiment and find what works for you. Some simple mantras are: 'Hong-Sau', 'So-Hum' and 'Om'.

Breathing exercises

Slowing and deepening your breathing is one of the fastest and quickest way to change your emotional state. Breathing exercises are useful when emotions are intense and our natural reaction is to freeze or hold our breath. Our breathing rate is usually unconscious, so when we take conscious control of our breath, we are also increasing integration between our conscious and unconscious minds.

Any simple breathing technique will do. The simple act of bringing your breath back into conscious awareness is helpful. Continuous breathing adds the extra component of preventing you from holding your inbreath, which is a common reaction to strong emotions. Breathe in on the count of five, then out again on the count of five. More breathing techniques are available on our blog www.cetfreedom.com

Exercise or move your body

You can change your emotional state by moving your body. Any exercise you enjoy will work – walking, dancing, jumping, running, cycling, swimming, weight training or any form of exercise. This has immediate short-term, as well as many longer-term, benefits for your brain chemistry and function.

Look up

According to neurolinguistic programming research, eye-accessing cues can reveal much about our mental, emotional and psychological state.[16] For instance, when we look down (and usually to the right), we are accessing emotions, feelings or thoughts. When we look *up*, we are accessing our vision and pulling ourselves out of our negative feelings and thoughts. You can transition emotions, thoughts and feelings by rolling your eyes up in their sockets so that you are looking towards your eyebrows. Don't strain or force it. Try it right now. Look up for a few moments and notice how you feel.

Peripheral vision

There are two ways to use your eyes. One is to see in foveal vision, using the centre of your visual field to see everything in detail. Although useful, this kind of gaze can trigger the sympathetic (stress) response. Bringing your awareness to your peripheral vision triggers the parasympathetic (relaxation) response. To access your peripheral vision, find something to look at that is about eye-level and in the mid-distance.

---

16. Richard Bandler, *The Ultimate Introduction to NLP*, revised edition (HarperCollins, 2013)

A little mark on the wall is perfect. In our trainings, I usually place a black cardboard spot on the wall with Blu Tack. Keep your eyes trained on that spot while you bring your awareness to the sides of your visual field. Remember to keep your eyes looking ahead – it's only your awareness that you're shifting. If you wear glasses, being aware of the frames is one way to do this. You can also hold your arms up to the sides of your face (not too close – think of the 'I surrender' pose) and wiggle your fingers while keeping your eyes gazing at your wall dot (or whatever point you have chosen).

Congratulations, you're now in peripheral vision. Notice your change of state. Apparently, it is impossible to hold onto a negative emotion when you are in peripheral vision.

Journaling

Journaling can be a helpful way to get painful thoughts out of your head and recorded so that your unconscious mind no longer needs to keep reminding you of them. Just remember that if you do it too much, you risk sliding into over-analysis or overly identifying with your problem.

Arts and crafts

Hobbies such as scrapbooking, creating art or other kinds of craft work have also been shown to have many benefits. Repetitive movements are meditative and have benefits similar to meditation. Crafting also gives you a sense of accomplishment, which can boost your mood.

The above is a brief list of things that can improve your emotional state. Remember that none of these are a replacement for using the full CET process, nor do they come close to the transformation possible when you do.

NINE

How To Help Someone In Emotional Pain

'You sound Australian, how did you come to live in England?' It's my first week in a new job. I'm technical manager at a Midlands manufacturing company meeting my new co-workers. It's been nearly five years since I escaped to freedom and this should be a simple enough question. I do sound Australian, and when I meet new people, I have two answers to this question.

The first answer is the sanitised version. I grew up in Australia and was sent to an English school to get a broader experience of education and the world. Most people like this answer. It implies that British education is superior to Australian and it satisfies some national pride. I learned to answer this way because almost any level of deeper personal information could lead to some quite awkward conversations. The other answer – that I had been groomed by a teacher at my previous school, persuaded to move in with him and then held as a virtual house prisoner – was so far out of their experience that they simply didn't know how to respond. It became apparent that most people simply couldn't understand my experience, or its impact on me. It made them uncomfortable. It might inspire pity or trigger their own trauma, but it was (and still is) rare for my story and experience to create a positive connection if shared too early in a relationship. I learned to present the sanitised and socially acceptable version first and only share my fuller experience when it was appropriate.

The sudden share

Have you been there? You're sitting across from, next to, or nearby someone dear to you. It can happen suddenly. No preamble and no readiness. The conversation is general, normal, about a movie or what you did during your last holidays. Suddenly, the room goes still. It becomes pregnant with anticipation. A silence might fall. Then they speak. It comes out blurted, or with pauses. Their voice is laden with emotion, pain and suffering:

'I think I was abused.'

'He hurt me.'

'I cut myself.'

The words might be different. They might be spoken in a myriad of different ways, but suddenly, there it is. Shared. It's out in the open. They've spoken. They have said the unsayable. Their heart seems to be in your hands. Now what do you do? What do you say? You care enough to get it right.

I can help you to help someone in pain, but before we go any further, let's be really clear: assisting someone to recover from trauma is a highly skilled and delicate task. Don't try to be their healer or therapist if you aren't trained to do so. Your role is different from that of a therapist or healer, and that's how it should be. There are things someone recovering from trauma can speak about with a therapist that they may never be able to share with you; but if your loved one is opening up, there are some empowering things you can do to support them. The techniques listed here work best as ways to soothe the person who is suffering temporarily; to experience permanent release, they will need to seek professional help.

From my years of research and work assisting thousands of clients to heal, it's become clear that much of the most common advice, suggestions and support we tend to offer not only fails, it actually makes them feel worse. Without the proper knowledge, training and understanding, we can do more harm than good, so the first way you can support someone recovering from past emotional pain is to learn how to avoid some common, unintentional faux pas.

What *not* to do

Avoid drama and making a fuss

This one may seem counterintuitive. For many of us, expressing shock, horror or outrage when someone tells us something shocking, horrifying or outrageous seems like the natural thing to do. We might say, 'Oh, no! How awful! Oh my God, what a terrible thing to have happened to you!' Well, what's wrong with that? A lot, as it turns out. When we express our shock or horror, we can amplify existing trauma. Being horrified makes the events horrifying. When we hear something like, 'Oh my God! How awful!' we're likely to think, 'Wow, this is a much bigger problem than I imagined. It must be a *really* big deal. I thought it was just a bad situation, but now it's a real tragedy.'

A dramatic reaction from someone else tells us how we 'should' feel about the situation rather than allowing us to feel whatever we actually feel, robbing us of our emotions. It applies meaning or judgement to a situation that we may not have even processed yet. When someone has been in an abusive situation, they may have been emotionally numb for years as a way to protect themselves from their abuser. It will take time – months or even years – for someone to begin to feel emotions (positive and negative) again. Until we know how someone feels about their abuse, everything we hear is just information. When we get emotional about someone else's emotions, we are diverting the attention back to ourselves. When our emotions are so big that they take up all the space, there's no space left for our loved one to feel seen and heard; to define and process their own emotions on their terms. This does not serve healing.

Avoid judgement of the victim, the abuser or the situation

It might seem obvious that we should avoid blaming someone for the trauma they've survived, but we need to be hyper-aware that nothing in our words or actions implies we are judging a loved one for their choices, behaviours or emotions. Trust me, they're already doing enough of that themselves.

We should also avoid expressing judgement around *what happened*. Ranting about injustice and cruelty and denouncing perpetrators can feel cathartic, but it does not help someone recovering from trauma. It's not our job to condemn or judge on behalf of our loved ones. Until someone has put meaning on the event for *themselves*, it's best to stay quiet and just listen.

Victims will often protect their abusers. This is not because they are stupid or because they liked being abused – they protect them because they genuinely believe they love and are loved. This is true when they are in the abusive situation, and after they have left (sometimes even years later). They will also protect their abuser to protect themselves from the shame of having chosen the situation. Refrain from joining in, even if your loved one starts to say negative things about their abuser. The danger of saying anything negative or judgemental about their abuser is that you might re-ignite their past loyalty and they will stop sharing.

Avoid pity

Our loved ones don't need or want our pity. Pity is disempowering. It puts you, the one doling out the pity, in the position of having more power. It tells them, subtly or overtly, that they are weak and worthy of pity. This robs them of the strength they'll need to recover and thrive.

Avoid being overly kind, helpful and/or supportive

Here's another one that may have you raising an eyebrow. Is there such a thing as being too supportive? Yes. When we are overly kind or sympathetic, we can create a dangerous emotional feedback loop in another person. The unconscious mind associates kindness with *the need* for kindness, and the person on the receiving end of our attentions can end up attaching meaning (the need for kindness) to a situation that might not have previously been associated with such a need (or any need at all).

Being too supportive makes a situation worse in three ways. First, we can interpret an overdose of kindness to mean that something is much worse than we had originally thought: 'If my friend is being so kind, something must *really* be wrong with me/the situation.' Secondly, overloading someone with offers of help and support suggests that someone *needs* support or needs the person offering it. This is disempowering, especially for people who may have been trapped in cycles of co-dependence. Likewise, kindness and showing love is part of the abusive cycle, and our seemingly innocent acts of too much kindness may well trigger them. In these scenarios, being too kind can be as uncomfortable as being unkind.

The best way we can support someone dealing with emotional pain from the past is to be matter of fact with our empathy. If someone asks for support, we are free to give it, but we should avoid suggesting or offering what hasn't been solicited.

Avoid physical touch

Under normal circumstances, physical contact with a loved one can be comforting and soothing, but this is not always the case for abuse survivors. Every physical touch, even on the most innocent place on the body, might trigger a muscle and emotional memory of being touched or harmed by their abuser. We may have no idea where on the body it's safe to touch, so hands off unless they instigate an embrace. The reason is that whenever someone is in a heightened emotional state, the nervous system hunts around for a cause. The nervous system will then connect, or anchor, the input it receives – a touch, a sound, a smell, etc – to the heightened emotion. This is what happens, neurologically, when our favourite song or a certain smell takes us back to a particular time in our lives. As we've all experienced, these kinaesthetic anchors can trigger both positive and negative memories and emotions.

When someone has experienced abuse or trauma, they may have dozens of kinaesthetic anchors all over their body, making physical touch a minefield of possible triggers for traumatic memories. Unfortunately, it is also possible for us to create new kinaesthetic anchors on someone else's body when our repeated touch becomes associated with emotional pain. For example, during funerals, it's common for people to touch the upper arm of the bereaved, setting an intense kinaesthetic anchor for grief in that part of the body. We can avoid firing or creating harmful associations by avoiding physical touch altogether or by asking for permission. Before going in for a hug or a touch, we can ask, 'Is it OK for me to give you a hug?' Don't be offended or take it personally if they say no. Remember, it's not about you.

Advice to avoid

'Stay positive'

Our society encourages us to believe that we can just 'positive think' any problem away. Unfortunately, this popular positive thinking movement masks what is, essentially, a form of spiritual and emotional gaslighting. Imagine you've broken your broken your leg and you're crying in agony on the pavement. How would you feel if a well-meaning passer-by leaned over you, smiled and said, 'Just stay positive?'

The same is true for emotional pain from the past. Not only does positive thinking not work, it negates the level of pain someone we are trying to help is experiencing. If that person has been in an abusive situation, they will have had their feelings negated by their abuser on a regular basis, because abusers often tell others how to feel emotionally. Our well-meaning words can end up sounding like echoes of abuse. It's not up to us to tell anyone else how they should, or should not, feel. When someone we want to help admits that they feel sad, miserable, angry, depressed, etc, we can affirm their feelings. We can tell them, 'OK. That's what you're feeling. Good.'

'Just let it go'

When we tell people that whatever happened in the past is in the past and it's time to 'just let it go', we are implying that releasing pain from the past is as simple as deciding to. We don't suggest to people that they should just cure the world of all known diseases, rid the world of cancer and solve world hunger and the energy crisis, do we? We don't expect even the most highly trained engineers, scientists and philosophers to solve these really complex things 'just like that'. 'Oh, and while you're about it – a colony on Mars would be nice, too ... ' Of course not, because it's not that simple.

Implied in the 'just let it go' imperative is the idea that someone is actively choosing to hold onto pain, and that when they 'just let it go', all their problems will float away by themselves. Then they will say to us, gratefully, 'Oh, silly me. Thank you so much for just telling me to let it go. Now my life has healed and you're my hero for telling me to let it go.' Let's face it – if it was so easy to 'just let it go', we would all be pain and trauma-free. None of us would experience emotional pain from the past. There are many neurological, ener-getic and psycho-spiritual reasons why we can't 'just let it go'. Emotional pain is complex, because it is installed at a neurological level deep in the unconscious mind. The emotional and energetic signature is locked in and it needs a process and a system to unlock and release it. Without a process, healing is like a fly banging its head against the windowpane, and that's a pain.

'Well, at least...'

...you have your health/a job/a home

...you're with a nice person now

...you have friends

...you're out

At least, at least, at least...Similar to positive thinking, affirmations like these negate pain. They suggest someone's feelings aren't valid by implying that because they have some good things, they have no right to feel bad. Removing a person's divine right to feel what they feel is a form of emotional gaslighting. The truth is, they already know what they have. They are *already* grateful for it, but all kinds of limiting beliefs might be making them feel unworthy or guilty for having these good things. Saying 'at least' will likely only make others feel *less* worthy and *more* ungrateful. At its worst, 'at leasting' someone we want to help demonstrates a lack of empathy, as if having a few 'good' things cancels out years of abuse and trauma. We wouldn't say, 'Oh, one of your children died, but at least you've got another.'

Don't make it about you

There are several ways that we can unintentionally turn someone else's story into our own tale of woe. We might say something like, 'That's just like what happened to me.' Imagine you are right on the cusp of sharing an incredibly painful story and suddenly someone interjects – 'Oh my God, the same thing happened to me. I had that as well, but I was abused earlier, and worse (or not as badly). Let me tell you about my experience...' That wouldn't feel so great, right? When we interrupt others, we move the energy and attention from them to ourselves. Even if we mean well and are trying to show solidarity, in practice, we can unintentionally make others feel unheard and unimportant.

We also divert the attention to ourselves when someone's trauma triggers us and we let the other person know it. We do this because we've let our own stuff become more important than our loved ones' stuff. In both situations, we make others feel invalidated and confused about who's supporting whom. They might feel burdened with the job of supporting *us* when they were asking for *our* support. They needed the space to open up, and we've just stepped in and moved them out of it. If our stuff and our past are still upsetting us, we aren't in the ideal place to help others. If we find ourselves confusing our pain with someone else's, it's time to get help for ourselves first, before helping someone else.

Finally, we should avoid sharing someone else's story or mentioning the role we've played in their healing journey. Maybe we feel we are justified in using someone's else trauma as a cautionary tale for others. Maybe we want to show someone what a good friend/family member we are. Maybe we want to prove to *ourselves* that we're a good person. Or maybe we're just a crisis-junkie who can't escape the thrill of having front-row seats to drama. Whatever our reason may be, our commitment to caring for and loving someone else is never – ever – for our own glory.

Never suggest that recovery is impossible

The belief that it's impossible to recover from trauma is pervasive in our culture. Science, specifically neuro-plasticity, has proven that the brain can reshape itself. If our brains can be trained to be suboptimal through trauma and abuse, they can also be positively reshaped with assistance and the right process.

When we tell someone that they'll 'just have to learn to live with' their trauma, we are telling them that they will never recover, which is an extremely limiting way to live. We end up worsening someone's emotional state when we say things like, 'Well, you'll just have to accept what happened to you and learn to cope, because it's with you forever. Those emotions will never go away. You'll have to learn to live with it.' All the variations of that sentiment are not only factually incorrect, they are disempowering.

How to help

If all those 'don'ts' have left you feeling like there's nothing you can do to help, I've got another 'don't' ... Don't despair. If you recognise actions you've taken in the past to help someone else, don't despair. I don't believe that anyone sets out to help people with the intention of doing more damage. If you've done any of the 'don'ts', know that you are forgiven and please forgive yourself. There are many ways to mindfully support someone recovering from emotional pain.

Ask

Instead of assuming we know best, or jumping in with advice and sympathy when we haven't been asked, we can ask: 'What do you need? How can I help?' Make it OK for someone to ask for help, and also be prepared to accept that they might not yet be ready or able to accept it.

Hold a safe space

When we are fully present for someone, without distractions or interruptions, we offer them a safe space for healing. Make time, privacy and space. Set boundaries on that time and space by telling others not to interrupt you. If you have small children, find a way for them not to be a distraction while you are trying to help someone.

Ensure the safety of the space by saying that you are OK with hearing anything someone may want to tell you. Be comfortable to say, 'I'm OK to hear anything you want to tell me, and whatever you do want to tell me, I will not share with anyone.' Confidentiality is key. Be curious and open-minded and ask some gentle opening questions to give them permission to share. For example, 'Would you like to talk more about that?' or, 'Is there anything else you want to share?'

Be comfortable with sitting in silence together if that's what someone needs.

Say thank you

Thanking them for sharing and trusting you makes them feel honoured and respected. It lets them know how much you appreciate them and their willingness to share by using a simple statement like, 'Thank you for trusting me enough to share this.'

Honour the changes they've already made

The fact that they are sharing with you means they have already made changes. The courage it takes to open up and share an experience is a huge step forward for anyone. It can be helpful for them if you recognise and acknowledge this and any other changes they have made.

Show respect

Show how much you respect them for any and all things they are doing or have achieved. If they have managed to leave an abusive situation, this is something to congratulate them for. Perhaps they are holding down a job or taking care of their family. For some people, just managing to get up, shower and dress most days is an achievement. You can be as specific or vague as you like. A great way to phrase this is to say something like, 'In light of all you've experienced, I have the greatest respect for you.' You could add, 'and how you've...' (include some observed behaviour that is empowering for them).

Tell them they have a support team

Just letting someone know that people are on their side is a powerful way to support them without disempowering them. Some good ways to express this are:

- 'I want you to know that you've got a big support team, and I'm on it.'

- 'I know that there will be a lot of people who would love, and be honoured, to support you through this.'

- 'I'm here for you.'

Believe in them and let them know it

Right now, they probably don't have much belief in themselves, but you can let them know that you believe in them. This is as simple as saying:

- 'I believe in you.'

- 'I know you're strong and can change what you need to.'

- 'I see your light.'

Know your role

Are you a friend or a therapist? (Hint: it's not easy be both.) If you feel like you're out of your league, ask: 'Is this something you might like to get help with? Would you like me to try and find some routes where you can get help?' It's likely that the person we want to help won't know where to look and they may also be ashamed of seeking out professional help.

A certified CET practitioner who knows how to create a bond with their client will feel completely safe to explore the sacred depths of their issues. Unless you've been trained to do this, no matter how well-meaning you are, it is best left to the professionals.

Consider training as a CET practitioner

You want to help. You are passionate about people's happiness and emotional wellbeing. Whether it's for yourself, a loved one, or because you would love to be there for others' loved ones in the same way you want someone to be there for yours, training to be a certified CET practitioner enables you to completely release all trauma, pain and negative emotions from the past.

TEN

What CET Can
And Can't Do

M y dad has some great phrases. They might seem superficial or obvious, but they have hidden wisdom. One such phrase is, 'Some people in this world are just arseholes; the trick is to spot them and stay away from them.'

Sophia and I had agreed to deliver a hypnosis certification training course together. The plan was that we would both market and sell places on the training. We agreed on a 60/40 split of any remaining profit, with the bigger portion to me as Sophia was brand new and had no experience of running a training course, whereas I had a decent email list, a brand, a website, terms and card payment facilities. One week before we were due to attend our course, we had only sold enough spots to cover the training costs for one of us. I say 'we', but, in reality, all the sales had come from my list and my marketing and sales efforts. I was still somehow persuaded that the person to lead the training was Sophia.

A few weeks later, we were making preparations to deliver the training to our group – organising the room, the chairs, all the things that needed to happen before the delegates arrived – and Sophia started renegotiating her cut. 'As I'm the lead trainer, and you're not qualified to run this, I think I should get the bigger cut. Let's face it, if I walked out now, you'd have to give everyone their money back. You couldn't run the course.' Wow. I hadn't expected this. She was right, of course – in a way. I took a deep breath and said,

'You have a point. Let me think about it.' Fortunately, the first delegates arrived and then we were underway. Throughout the training, Sophia treated me like her assistant, asking me to arrange coffees for the delegates, snacks for her, run errands, organise her slides for her presentation and even look after her little dog. I complied for the sake of keeping the peace. I was becoming pissed off with her attitude, but I was a master of state management and no one knew how I felt. I decided to chalk this up to experience, not work with her again, and prepare much better joint agreements in future.

The next week, I sent her the spreadsheet with the costs and profit. In my email I told her she could invoice for the 40% portion of the profit. The phone rang a few moments later. It was Sophia. 'The number is wrong and I think I can see what you've done. You've mistakenly given yourself the 60% instead of me.'

'This is the right number,' I replied.

'No, we agreed at the venue that I would get 60%.'

'I know you asked for this, but I don't recall agreeing to it. Do you have any written record of this new agreement?' She didn't, but I did: I had a copy of the email exchange in which we had agreed the 60% to my company. She wasn't happy about this, and as she continued to argue with me, I told her that this was completely unreasonable and unprofessional behaviour. Not only had she brought in *zero* sales to the whole project, but she had also behaved appallingly by trying to renegotiate her fee only moments before the delegates were due to arrive – essentially blackmailing me. She was quiet for a moment. When she spoke again, her tone was placating and patronisingly soft.

'I can feel your pain. I think you're being triggered. Is this your past trauma or scarcity thinking coming up? Shall we clear this so we can move past it?'

'No, I'm not being triggered,' I declared. 'You are, in fact, behaving like an arsehole. I will pay the amount originally agreed and we will end our professional association.'

Here was one situation that needed a resolution in which CET had no part.

The truth about CET

If the emotions you feel are an appropriate response to an ongoing situation or current behaviour by another, then nothing will be able to release them – and quite rightly so. CET is great, but it does have some limitations. Let's explore them together and consider some common questions. This the 'troubleshooting' part of your manual on the human experience!

CET treats the cause, not the symptoms

If you have a problem in your life, the chances are it is a symptom of a deeper, hidden cause. For example, let's say you have a problem with money. You find yourself being underpaid, often struggling with money or in debt. Your bank account is empty. This is the result of any number of possible limiting beliefs that cause you to make poor money choices. You can't use CET to release 'I'm broke' – you need to find what is causing you to create the situation where you repeatedly find yourself being broke. Likewise, if you hold feelings of deep unworthiness or limiting beliefs about being unlovable, then you are unlikely to get yourself onto the dating scene. If you meet someone you are attracted to, you might not ask them out or you might not accept an invitation to meet for coffee because you assume they'll only find out later that you're a truly terrible human, so you're better off saying no now. You'll remain alone and prove yourself right, but you can't release the experience of being alone – you need to find the beliefs that are causing that situation to become manifest.

CET works fast, regardless of how long you've been suffering

The duration of a problem you want to target with CET has no relationship to how quickly and easily the resistance to love can be released. Think of it like this: if you have a stone in your shoe, the length of time that it's been in your shoe doesn't make it harder to remove.

CET heals emotional pain from the past

If CET were a time machine, it could only ever travel back in time, never into the future. That's because CET can only release emotions from the past. Emotions are only a problem if we feel pain in the present as a result of events in the past. If you're thinking, 'But Lisa, I feel really crappy now. Why can't CET eliminate all the negative feelings I'm feeling today?' then let's go back to the purpose and function of emotions that we discussed in Chapter 2. We want to still feel any emotions caused by our present situation, because, like a barometer, they reflect the highs and lows of our emotional states. Emotions let us know when we are on or off track, when we're moving towards or away from our desires. We need them.

Even if we could release painful emotions that don't serve us, we wouldn't want to. That's like turning off the fire alarm telling you to get out of a burning building. Yes, it solves the 'problem' of that noise giving you a headache, but you're still trapped in a burning building. If you're in the wrong job, a shitty relationship, being bullied or in an abusive situation, it is absolutely essential that your emotions let you know that you need to take action to change your present circumstances.

CET releases emotions that we are conscious of

CET can only release what we are conscious of – hence the name, Conscious Emotional Transformation. If it's not conscious, you can't release it. That's why it's so important to identify the root cause of pain. Sometimes, the cause of our pain is so deeply unconscious that we don't even know it's there. The only reason we know something isn't working is because we keep repeating the same negative experience (a string of unfulfilling jobs or lousy partners, for example). We know that there must be a reason why we keep losing money or dating jerks, but we can't figure it out. The likely reason is a limiting belief from the past that needs to be released, but we need to have that belief in our conscious awareness in order for CET to release it. That doesn't mean that CET can't work for you. A certified CET coach will have the skills and training to bring the root cause of negative emotions and limiting beliefs into your awareness.

'But I can't feel my emotions!' Is this you, lovely reader? Have you ever felt like you just can't access your feelings? Do you feel like you hit a wall when you try to 'get into' your emotions? It's likely that you've trained yourself to suppress or deny your feelings through socialisation ('boys don't cry' or 'girls should be sweet' and other rubbish). Good news: you don't need to feel your emotions. You just need to be aware of them. CET requires good rapport, communication and integration between the unconscious and the conscious minds. If you are the kind of person who works from a logical, analytical and rational place, and who likes to work things out (I see you, fellow logic-and-reason types), it's possible that you don't trust your unconscious mind. It might be difficult for you to bring your emotions into your awareness and find the triggers. Your highly trained conscious mind can shut out your unconscious mind, blocking the flow of information. With the communications shut down between them, you won't be able to bring whatever it is you need to bring into your conscious awareness so that CET can do the necessary repair work. You might find that doing some exercises such as simple breathing exercises or meditation to increase rapport between your unconscious and conscious minds will really help create a sense of trust and mutuality between them. Again, working with a CET coach can also really help you develop the relationship between your unconscious and conscious minds.

Frequently asked questions

I have suffered significant trauma. Can CET work on severe trauma victims?

Yes, CET is ideal for trauma. CET is an incredibly powerful process and works on even the deepest traumas (eg, PTSD, long-term and damaging sex/child/relationship abuses). CET works the same way for serious trauma as it does for small trauma. On the neurological level, damage to the flow of love energy is just that – a break or block that needs repair. While one person might come to CET to heal from sexual assault and another to get over a fear of public speaking, the neurological damage is the same. There's no difference between the process of repairing. In some ways, the repairing is the easy part for serious trauma victims. What can be harder is feeling safe enough to bring deep, painful emotions into awareness. I strongly advise victims of serious trauma to work with a practitioner when you decide to try CET.

How will I know if CET has worked?

You will know that CET has worked because you won't be triggered, and you won't feel the negative emotion.

Is it possible to feel worse after CET?

Yes, it's possible for CET to bring up old, long-repressed emotions that your unconscious mind had buried to keep you safe. What you are feeling is not a new feeling though. It was always there, just not in your conscious awareness. Now that you know how to release negative emotions from the past by bringing them into your awareness, you can use CET to release any ugly stuff that may have been dragged up from your deep, unconscious mind.

Once I've released a negative emotion from the past with CET, is it possible for that emotion to come back?

People can feel as if a negative emotion has come back if they are confusing an old emotion with a new one. You can identify if what you are feeling is an old or new emotion by keeping track of your triggers and seeing if they are the same as, or different from, your old triggers. It's also possible for the unconscious mind to keep releasing emotion into your awareness. This is a *good* thing. It means that your unconscious mind is no longer repressing the emotion, and the communication between your unconscious and conscious minds is healthy. You can repeat CET as many times as you need until all of the emotion has been brought into your awareness and the resistance to love it created has been removed.

I suffer from chronic pain/disease/illness.
Can CET heal my physical ailments?

I have been asked if CET can release something like cancer or a physical illness. The answer is no. CET can't release physical pain or cure the physical problem causing it. CET only works on the emotional or energetic cause of physical pain. That doesn't mean you can't use CET to help the healing process. Remember, physical pain is the pain we feel when we are ill or injured. The purpose of this pain is to encourage us to stay still, conserve energy and rest, until we are well enough to prevent further injury. You *can* use CET to remove any limiting beliefs you might have about your diagnosis, prognosis and ability to heal. It usually requires deeper work with a certified CET practitioner to understand the emotional or energetic causes of physical pain.

Is there any reason why CET
wouldn't work for me?

I've been doing versions of CET for years. One thing has held true in every setting and every format and every version of Conscious Emotional Transformation. Success requires attention. CET won't work if you do it at the gym while running on the treadmill. It won't work for you if you don't complete the written exercises before each step. If won't work for you if you try it while your mind is partially focused on something else (the kids, getting dinner ready, work or whatever it is that distracts you from being 100% present). To bring an emotion into awareness, you must be looking at it, feeling it and paying attention to it – all things that require your full concentration. To repair and release the emotion, you also need to be actively participating in the process. CET is not a guided meditation where you just sit back and all your worries float off into the ether. CET only works when you actually *do* it and follow the instructions.

Don't stand in the way of CET

CET can only release what you're willing to let go of

Before every release, I ask if all aspects of the client's being are willing to let go of the problem. It may seem surprising, but sometimes, much as we might *say* we want to let go of the pain from the past, there is a part of us that also wants to hold on to it. Sometimes, through habit, we feel safe in our cages. It could also be possible that some of our problems are also serving us.

No surrender

I was working with a client who wanted to find and release a limiting belief that was stopping her from recovering fully from a long-standing illness. To my surprise, the client said no. She was not willing to release the problem. Digging deeper, we discovered that if she did let go of the problem, she would be expected to resume housework and cooking, which she hated. Of course, we then worked on the issues and limiting beliefs that caused her to think that she had to do the housework. (It turned out that there aren't any 'rules' that say all woman have to do housework unless they are sick…) Once we'd released that set of limiting beliefs, she was free to choose to stay ill, or to recover. She chose to recover.

Follow the instructions

One of the biggest stumbling blocks to the success of a CET session is when someone makes assumptions about how CET works. Clients frequently expect CET to be similar to something else they have tried and perhaps assume that they know what it's about and don't need too much guidance. If you've ever spent any time observing someone attempting to assemble flat-pack furniture while resolutely refusing to open the instruction book, you will understand what I mean here. You can hinder CET by:

- Trying to understand the problem

- Trying to remember the events, the order and sequence and all the details of the trauma

- Trying to understand why things happened

- Trying to take away, let go of or remove the emotion or energy

- Forcing or trying to make the emotions go away

- Trying to 'think positively' rather than simply bringing the emotions into awareness

- Analysing the problem through applying complex psychological labels, diagnoses and theories to the trigger, trauma, response or situation. (None of this seems to actually remove the resistance to love)

- Trying to 'fill up' the 'empty space' with positive energy, white light or similar

All of these can actually prevent the CET process from working its magic. CET is different from other healing techniques. It requires an active *un*-learning and a willingness to let go of our expectations and assumptions.

CET works. Not only will you experience yourself as if you were never damaged, you'll experience yourself as whole and complete. You'll find entirely new ways of being and of expressing yourself. Situations that took conscious effort to handle before will become effortless and joyful. Situations that were previously painful or unbearable become simply events – memories and information without the emotional charge. CET creates a new paradigm for healing. It is radical and revolutionary, a powerful tool for raising our collective consciousness and embodying the highest and truest versions of our divine selves. CET serves profound and lasting change.

So, what would the world look like if we all embraced Conscious Emotional Transformation?

ELEVEN

A World CETfree

Some of my daughter's friends were recently discussing a schoolmate who wanted to go to uni to learn languages but had performed badly on some exams in the past – and she has unsupportive parents. 'She thinks she's not good enough for uni,' said Ella. I was itching to say, 'She just needs to do CET,' because the truth is, with a single session, Ella could release all the pain of her past failures – all those limiting beliefs and decisions she might have installed. She would be empowered and motivated to go to uni. Would she get into uni easily? Maybe. Maybe not, but at least she'd be in a position to *try*. Every day, I observe conversations and stories like this and want to say, 'Just do CET.' Sometimes I do; sometimes I stay quiet.

Breaking free

Painful emotions and limiting beliefs can influence every choice and decision we make – if we let them. It's too easy to simply suggest that changing our beliefs is a simple matter of making a choice. We all know it's not that easy. Just saying, 'Believe in yourself,' is useless, because when we inevitably fail, we end up feeling even worse about ourselves.

On top of that, almost every novel, movie, news story and social media post tells us that it's impossible to recover from trauma. Our culture(s) repeatedly tells us, in a variety of ways, that we have to learn to live with pain and with trauma, and that maybe, just maybe, after a long time and a lot of external reassurance and expensive therapies, the problem might just become manageable. That the best you can hope for is to learn to live with trauma, spend your life trying to avoid triggers and psyching yourself up for events that are will be forever challenging due to your trauma.

What if that weren't true? What would the world be like if we weren't all in emotional pain? What would it be like to have the resilience to stand up to the challenges we all face at times in our lives, confident that we could move on from them at peace with ourselves?

CET and grief and loss

It's normal to grieve for our lost loved ones. Our ERC is stimulated by loss and should, in a perfect world, complete its natural cycle. We think about our loss, act on our grief in culturally appropriate ways and learn from the experience, but many of us experience problems when we grieve for an extraordinarily long time or never seem to get over the passing of a loved one. Usually this happens when something is unresolved; there is some unfinished business. We might replay times when we wished things had gone differently. Often, this manifests as anger, hurt or guilt and our negative emotions become tied up in the sadness of loss.

RELEASING REGRET

Dana simply couldn't get over the death of her mother. A few weeks before her mother had died, she'd invited Dana out to celebrate her birthday, but Dana had turned her down. When I asked her why, Dana took a deep breath and then, through tears, 'It's a bit sad isn't it, spending your birthday with your mum?'

I was starting to understand. Feeling sad at the loss of someone we love is normal, but we know something has gone awry if, nearly a decade later, they are still grieving to this depth. When this happens, it's usually because there is some unfinished business. Dana had actually come to see me hoping I would use my mediumship skills to contact her mum and ask her for her forgiveness. I knew from experience that this might seem to be the solution, but it rarely worked in practice. Instead, we used CET to allow her to release what she described as 'oceans of guilt'. In the part of the process where she accessed the new learnings and meaning, she had an awareness of her mother's presence.

'I could feel her. She seemed to be telling me it was all alright. She knew I loved her. She knows I love her. She's forgiven me. She wants me to forgive myself.'

'Can you do that now?' I asked.

'Yes. It's as if there's nothing to forgive. Mum was actually happy for me; that I had so many friends and was living such a happy life. I feel she wants me to do that again.'

'Well of course she does. She loved you then and loves you now, and love means you want that person to be happy and to live a happy life.'

CET allows us to clear these emotions, remove these blocks and resistances to love, leaving only love for our lost loved ones. We may still feel sad, but the sadness becomes a joyful sadness. The joy of having known and loved this person becomes more significant than the other, negative emotions.

CET and forgiveness

One of the most common questions I get asked about my past is, 'Have you forgiven him?' When I say, 'Yes,' they ask, 'How did you do it?'

WHO IS POWERFUL NOW?

'Do you want me to walk with you?' Rachel asked as she pulled up outside an average-looking terraced house in north London.

'No,' I replied. 'We might need to leave quickly; you're my getaway driver.' Keeping my breathing deliberately deep and steady, I stepped out of the car and walked to the flat. I stared at the door. I looked up at the first-floor window. I could see a scratching-tree and other cat toys. It looked so innocuous. It was hard to imagine so much had happened to me behind those panes of glass. Behind that door were the stairs I'd heard my abuser tread. When the key turned in that lock (was it still the same one?), my heart would start to race as I'd braced myself for the evening's onslaught.

I was visiting the Knitting and Stitching Show with a good friend and while we were lounging in the Airbnb a few nights before, I mentioned to her that I thought we must close to where I'd been held. I checked on my phone's map: thirteen minutes' drive.

'Do you want to go?' Rachel asked.

'I think I do,' I said. I wanted to see what it felt like now. I stood and stared. It had been years since I had last been there. This was one of the two properties in which I had been held as a house prisoner. Gazing at the door, the window, remembering all that had happened. I checked in with myself. How *did* I feel now?

'He's got nothing on me.' I realised the full empowerment of this moment. I could be here, at the place where I was held, and feel OK. Not triggered. I felt fine. I felt better than fine. I felt strong, with an overwhelming sense of freedom and power. To think that I could be here, witnessing the energy of the walls, the bricks, the path, the wood frame of the door. I took a deep breath and pictured that younger me in the back room, in the lock-in, praying to be rescued. I saw that younger me and said to her, loudly and clearly: 'Lisa! No one is coming!' My past self had got the message, because even though I hadn't known then if, or how, I would get out, I had gone anyway.

Here's my take on forgiveness. The only reason we might feel the need to forgive someone, whom we believe has wronged us in some way is because we think that wrong has damaged us in some way. I do not believe that I am damaged or broken as a result of being with Gary. I spend almost no time thinking about him or my past. The only reason I do speak about my past is in the context of talking about CET and what's possible. It's true that I might be a different person if I had I not been kept as a house prisoner, but I know there's nothing wrong with me. If you and I were ever to meet, I bet you'd realise pretty quickly that I'm awesome – I believe that everyone loves me, they just might not realise it yet!

I live a joy-filled life. I have a wonderful husband and family. At the time of writing, I'm about to become a grandma. My life isn't 'perfect', yet every day unfolds perfectly, offering me a range of experiences. Some I enjoy; others I dislike and either take action to change (if it's within my control), or I simply wait until they have passed. I do not experience myself or my life as damaged or broken. If I did, I would take steps to change it.

Antibiotics for the soul

Before the invention of antibiotics, anaesthetics, vaccines and other modern medicine, the human race lived precariously. Any individual, no matter their status, wealth or class could (and likely would) be struck down and killed by diseases that have either now been almost eradicated by vaccines or that can be cured easily.

If you get sick today, modern medicine, though imperfect, has treatments that range from simply making you more comfortable or extending your life, to curing or healing you completely. The treatments available today, despite their flaws, would seem like a miracle to people just a few generations ago. It might seem grandiose to suggest that CET could have the same impact on our mental health. So far, all that many can expect is to be told to live with their problems, but could CET be to mental health what antibiotics and vaccines have been to physical health?

Imagine

Imagine a world where everyone had access to CET. Imagine a world where no one had to waste energy holding onto and managing their pain. Imagine a world CETfree...How would we live?

Here's my radical proposition to you: what if what we really seek is joy?

Joy is the experience of love flowing freely throughout our being. Joy comes from within and is independent of our external experiences. Joy doesn't deny that material and external factors (such as unemployment, being dumped or experiencing a global pandemic) affect us – it simply uses them as feedback, much like a ship's navigation system informs the captain if it's headed off course. When we are free from resistance to love, we know that pain is just that feedback. Unlike happiness, we can experience joy at the same time that we experience a negative emotion. That's right – we can even feel joy when we're in pain. We might be feeling uncomfortable, but that's the point. The pain exists to give us the information we need so we can take appropriate action.

The experience of joy does not require a choice between the material and the spiritual. Joy embraces *both*. Joy allows us to be fully present to what is present and respond to it in empowering and effective ways without descending into pain. This is not only possible but is also how we are intended to live. CET enables joy (not happiness), but what would a joy-*full* world look like and how might it affect some of life's inevitable challenges? Joy is:

- The absence of suffering

- The absence of resistance to love

- The absence of trauma

- Love energy flowing freely throughout our entire being

A world CETfree

CET raises consciousness. It raises the consciousness of the whole planet. What would a conscious, awakened world look like? Imagine a world that's free from hatred, from ego, from greed and fear and lack. Imagine a world free from racism, sexism or prejudice. After all, the root of all of these must surely be resistance to love?

Imagine an infinite world; an infinite universe. This is a world where everyone makes their choices and lives their lives from their own highest self. Imagine this at every level – from corporates to government, parents, teachers, partners, passers-by – all living from, and acting from, their infinitely loving, highest selves. This is a world that we fill with the highest form of love: the kind of love that empowers every individual to grow and expand and become more love – to be love and loved and loving, and to know it consciously. *This* is the real prize.

Conclusion

I wrote this book in the midst of a global pandemic. As I typed these words, danger and uncertainty were increasing daily. One thing we know without a doubt: the world is riddled with challenges and problems, uncertainty and pain. Climate change, inequality, discrimination, bullying, increasingly divided societies, war... We are experiencing a global moment when people, young and old, feel disconnected from themselves and each other.

We have the technology and resources to solve problems such as climate change, hunger, inequality and extreme poverty. The reason we haven't yet isn't due to lack of knowledge or technology: it's a lack of political or social pressure – what I call a lack of emotional motivation. We don't share resources across the globe because of fear. We fear that others won't support us if we are in need, so we hoard resources. The reason we (as a species and as societies) haven't solved our global problems all links to trauma.

Almost every problem that we see in the world is the result of unresolved trauma. I'm aware this seems like a grand statement but let's consider... We don't need to spend long on either mainstream or social media to see how reactive people are. People are triggered and acting out from pain and hurt. We can practically *see* their broken emotional response cycles looping. We can observe inappropriate emotional responses in others as they speak, act and respond to the actions of others. Judgement, hatred, fear, anger, hurt and shame are acted out all the time, in full view of anyone with a social media account or TV.

Alongside this, we have the eternal struggle to get ahead, get security, get enough money, get more money, get a house, get a better house, get the even bigger house, get the guy or the girl, get the job, get the better job, get the car, get the body, get *something*... The cynic in me sometimes wonders if this is a by-product of late-stage capitalism. We buy more stuff that we don't need when we are in emotional pain. The beauty industry is a perfect example of this. It's a multi-billion-dollar industry that profits from our lack of confidence. It tells us that we won't be loved because our lips aren't juicy enough, our skin not fair enough, our thighs not thin enough, our eyebrows not quite the right shape or our abs not chiselled enough. However, if we buy this or that product for only £49.99, we might just pass for good enough (and we'll have to buy it every month forever)…This example could translate across many industries. Maybe it benefits someone for us be in pain? Now, this could just be a limiting belief that I hold about society, but it's still worth asking the question and running the thought experiment. All of what we might call the consequences of consumerism or capitalism are rooted in the quest for happiness.

Yet, deep down, even if it's outside of our conscious awareness, most of us know that none of these things create or produce happiness. In fact, many spiritual teachings suggest that the path to joy or enlighten-ment or nirvana is to relinquish our desires for all the material things we've attached to happiness. We may have been taught that pursuing our desires leads us off the path of enlightenment, so we should release our attachments to our desires. It's simply not possible to be alive and not have desires. Seeking and wanting are a fundamental part of the human condition. If we are alive, we will desire to *stay* alive. This isn't unspiritual; this is not a sign of lack of enlightenment. Why should nirvana come at the cost of giving up the career we've worked hard for or a healthy, life-giving relationship? Why can't we experience fulfilment without sacrifice?

Most societies teach us that happiness comes from the outside. It's the result of us getting our desires met. If we are happy, we should not experience suffering. In fact, if we experience a negative emotion, we must be doing something wrong – we are not doing whatever thing we should be doing to achieve our happiness. Yikes! That's a tough situation. Not only are we dependent on external factors for our happiness, but if we aren't happy, then the blame lies within ourselves. Instead of simply noticing the negative emotion as important emotional information, we start to attach meaning and significance to the current situation. We must be failures, lazy, unworthy, victims or sinners. Similarly, spiritual dogma labels negative emotions as 'bad' and to be avoided, forcibly pushed aside and replaced by 'higher vibrations'.

How many of you, dear Readers, have been told to move away from the bad and towards the blissful, loving, higher, positive, more 'spiritual' ways of being? To deny what is present in the physical world because it's unpleasant is like putting a smiley sticker on the fuel gauge telling us we need to take action. It's nothing more than a method of dissociation. It denies us not only our pain, but also our joy. That's a lot of pressure and expectation. It's a teaching that fell especially flat while I was writing this book. It's all very well to tell us to 'seek a higher vibration', but how do we achieve happiness while facing a real and tangible threat of a dangerous disease? Under these terms, happiness doesn't sound so happy, does it?

Imagine a world where anyone who becomes aware of resistance or emotional pain can become free of this. Almost instantaneously.

Imagine a world CET free. Better still: let's create a world CET free!

I know that CET works. It reCETs you to joy. It reCETs us all to a place of potential, where we can be, do and have more of what we want, and also enjoy the journey towards experiencing it.

Next steps

Dear Reader, I was going to start this part by asking, 'Did you enjoy reading my book?' but perhaps that's the wrong question. Better questions might be: 'Did it resonate with your soul? Did some of its lessons help light up painful past experiences in such a way that they now feel easier for you?' I'd like to open this conversation and hear from you. I'd love to hear from you. If you're willing to share, you can interact with me by connecting with me on social media (see links at the end of The Author); or if you'd rather have a private conversation, head over to my site www.cetyourselffree.com where you'll find an email.

It's my wish for you that you found this book enlightening, and that it awakened in you hope and a desire for change – change that you now feel is more possible and easier for you achieve. No amount of talking *about* CET can replace actually experiencing it for yourself. If you're ready to give CET a try, head over to www.cetfreedom.com You can also get completely free access to the self-healing version of CET, info on how to contact a certified practitioner, how to join our community to get further support, or take the trauma heat map to identify how trauma is impacting your life.

Glossary

Block

A block is any resistance to love. It is a metaphor for describing how our neurological pathways can become blocked, damaged or constricted by trauma. As a result of blocks, we feel anger, sadness, guilt, hurt and/or fear.

Conscious Emotional Transformation (CET)

A psycho-spiritual technology that removes all and any resistance to love, leaving the individual healed, whole and trauma-free.

Co-dependency

A relationship where each partner has excessive emotional or psychological reliance on the other. It is usually an unhealthy relationship, as each attempt to become whole through the other, rather than experiencing wholeness from within.

Conscious mind

The part of us that experiences reality; it's also the part of us that chooses and decides what's real. Our conscious mind is everything we pay attention to in our present moment of awareness. It allows us to focus and concentrate; it is the home of rational thought, judgements, decisions and assessments. It is our free will. The conscious mind isn't fixed; our present moment of awareness can change at any moment and can move between our past (memories), our immediate present moment and our future (hopes, dreams, fears, etc).

Emotional response cycle (ERC)
The four-step cycle of how we respond to external stimuli. The four steps are:

- Stimulus: The external event, situation or circumstance which triggers the ERC.

- Thought: The meaning we attribute to the event.

- Feeling: The internal feelings which create the emotional response. Sometimes the terms feeling and emotion are used interchangeably, but emotion is better described as the label we give to the feeling-thought experience.

- Action: The final step in the ERC are the actions we take or the external behaviour we display.

Resistance
An opposition by a slowing force. In the context of CET, we refer to resistance as what resists, stops or prevents love from flowing through our nervous system. Resistance in the context of CET is not to be confused with electrical resistance.

Response
A reaction to something. This also forms part of the description of the ERC, which describes how an external stimulus leads, via our internal thoughts, feelings and emotions, to a behaviour or action.

Source
The indefinable experience of that which is beyond ourselves. Some might call it God, others might describe it as an energy, others might refer to it as the super-consciousness. Yet others might simply explain it as 'that which we cannot know'. How you describe or experience this is up to you.

Stimulus
Step 1 of the ERC: the external event, circumstances or stimulus that starts the emotional response cycle and sets it running.

Trauma
An event or series of events that installs a block or resistance to love in the neurology. In the context of CET, we refer to this as any set of experiences that leaves a lasting negative impact on the individual. If you have blocks, we consider this to be trauma, and it's this that CET can release so easily.

Trigger
An event in the present that produces an emotional reaction caused by trauma or blocks from past events. The past is still impacting the present and future.

Unconscious mind
The unconscious mind is the opposite to the conscious mind and represents all that you are *not* aware of. Our unconscious mind contains our personal programming, beliefs and patterns, emotional blueprints, strategies and skills. While these things are usually completely outside of our awareness, we manifest their effects in our choices, beliefs and behaviours. Memories and emotions reside in the unconscious mind, including unresolved emotions and trauma from the past.

Acknowledgements

Writing this book has been one of the most difficult pieces of work I have undertaken to date – even more than my PhD thesis. I found it challenging to balance the technical explanations and theory with the sensitive message of this work. What seemed like such a simple idea, to 'write a book about CET', became a two-year saga where work on this book not only wriggled into almost every day, but also into my thoughts even when not at my desk.

I am eternally grateful to every therapist, coach and mentor I have worked with. Not only this book but also CET itself would not have been created without you – especially Tad and Adriana James, Eliana Harvey, Marcia Karp, Wendy Salter, David Shephard, Richard Asimus, Kevin Nations, Dr Joanna Martin, Elizabeth Purvis and many more. You know who you are. Thank you!

I would like to acknowledge the genius of Sara Price in assisting me to name the process.

To Jenn Reimer: I am grateful to have had the opportunity and privilege of working with you, Jenn. I could not have finished this book without your guidance, support and expertise in structuring the content and shaping my stories so that they are easy to read, yet still maintain their power throughout the chapters. Your advice on how to convey the complex concepts in the book was invaluable. Without you, this book would never have got beyond the first few chapters.

To each and every one of my clients who has ever worked with me: you are, and always will be, my biggest teachers. I am in awe of your willingness to go to the places you were terrified of so that you could heal. The world is a better place because you chose bravery over fear.

I am hugely grateful to Rachel Sampson, who, when I was on the point of abandoning the book, read it and shared with me the impact it had had on you. Hearing how this book inspired you, Rachel, and changed your mindset was the encouragement I needed at the perfect time and made all of those hours spent wrestling with the book worthwhile. I think every author should have at least one person like you around so they don't give up!

Thanks to everyone on the Dent global team and at Rethink Press, especially Verity, for refining the manuscript with your fresh eyes.

Thanks must also go to my team at MindCET Ltd, for holding the space and protecting my time while I worked on this book.

A special mention to Kathryn Mackellar, your friendship and support is so precious to me.

Thank you to my husband and all my family for all the love, inspiration and support you bring me every day.

The Author

Having freed herself from the trauma of being imprisoned for five years from the age of fifteen by a paedophile, Lisa Turner made a radical transition: from scientist with a PhD in mathematical modelling and aero-acoustics to therapist and teacher of consciousness. She is dedicated to supporting others to free their minds from limiting beliefs and emotional pain, as well as from trauma on all levels.

Lisa trained in numerous modalities, including neurolinguistic programming, western mystery, eastern mystery, life coaching, hypnosis, psychology, yoga, Huna, Shamanism, tarot, tantra, chakras, Reiki, EFT and EmoTrance before successfully developing a therapy, Conscious Emotional Transformation (CET), that enables you to let go of the past and lead a life free from emotional pain. CET heals in a matter of hours what other therapies might take years to achieve (if they ever do).

Lisa is driven to combine science and spirituality. In doing so, she builds models using scientific tools and teaching to test, prove and gain evidence on spiritual therapies in her cutting-edge work.

The author of five books, a speaker and trainer, Lisa has a team of coaches who use Conscious Emotional Transformation in both groups and on a one-to-one basis. Her mission is simple: to enable individuals to become self-actualised, fully empowered, internally driven and motivated, and to create tangible, real-world results by elevating consciousness.

Originally from Melbourne, Australia, Lisa now lives in Cornwall with her husband, daughter and many pets. Home is where she can paint, swim, cycle, bake cakes and knit jumpers. Lisa is healed, and you can be too.

CET is available on many levels, and there is a free home-study course, group coaching and 1:1 sessions available. Lisa also trains practitioners and coaches to use CET with their own clients. To find out more about how you could train to be a certified CET practitioner or just learn more about CET, head over to www.cetfreedom.com

- ⓕ ww.facebook.com/cetfreedom
- 🔲 www.linkedin.com/in/liturner/
- 🔲 ww.linkedin.com/company/cetfreedom
- 🔲 https://twitter.com/DrLisaTurner
- ✉ lisaturner@cetfreedom.com

Lightning Source UK Ltd.
Milton Keynes UK
UKHW020759180822
407484UK00007B/516